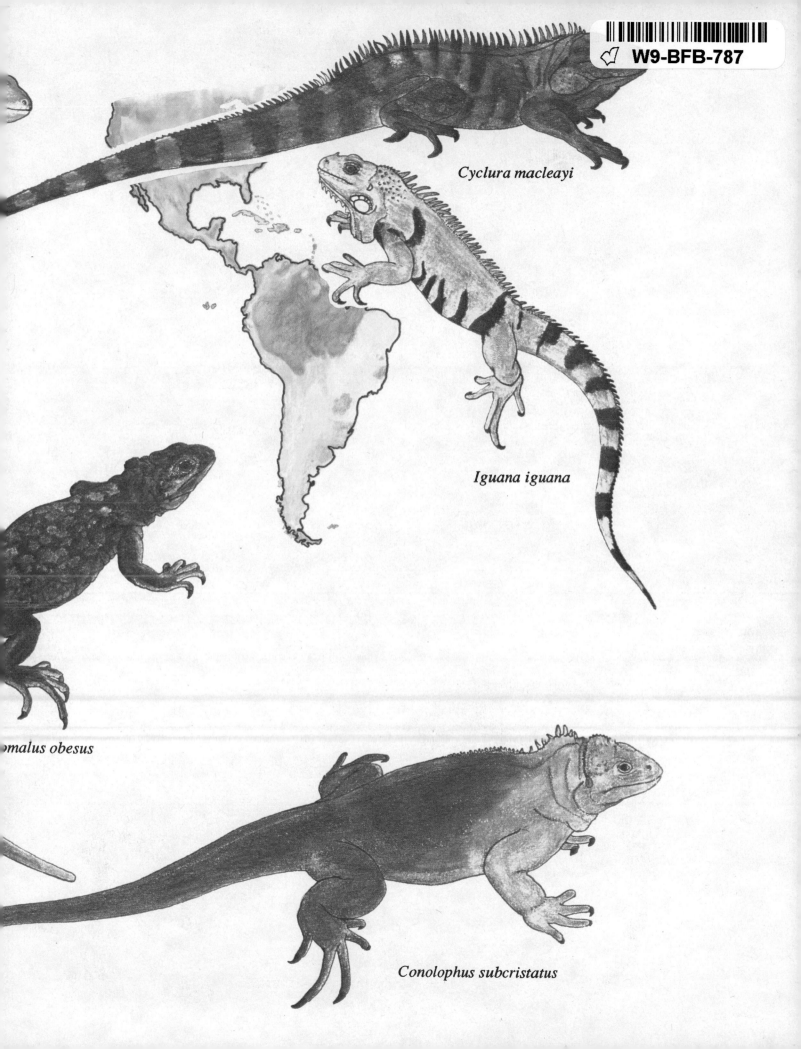

Cyclura macleayi

Iguana iguana

Conolophus subcristatus

malus obesus

Iguanas:

A Guide to Their Biology and Captive Care

Fredric L. Frye, B.Sc., D.V.M., M.Sc., CBiol, FIBiol

Fellow, Royal Society of Medicine

and

Wendy Townsend

Krieger Publishing Company
Malabar, Florida
1993

Original Edition 1993

Printed and Published by
KRIEGER PUBLISHING COMPANY
KRIEGER DRIVE
MALABAR, FLORIDA 32950

FROM A DECLARATION OF PRINCIPLES JOINTLY ADOPTED BY A COMMITTEE OF THE AMERICAN BAR ASSOCIATION AND A COMMITTEE OF PUBLISHERS:

This publication is designed to provide accurate and authoritative information in regard to the subject matter covered. It is sold with the understanding that the publisher is not engaged in rendering legal, accounting, or other professional service. If legal advice or other expert assistance is required, the services of a competent professional person should be sought.

Library of Congress Cataloging-in-Publication Data
Frye, Fredric L.
    Iguanas: a guide to their biology and captive care/Fredric L. Frye and Wendy Townsend.—Original ed.
        p. cm.
    Includes bibliographical references (p.   ) and index.
    ISBN 0-89464-695-8 (acid-free paper)
    1.   Iguanas as pets. 2. Iguana. 3.   Captive reptiles.
    I. Townsend, Wendy. II. Title.
        SF459.I38F78 1992
        639.3'95—dc20

10   9   8   7   6   5   4   3   2

CONTENTS

DEDICATION

To Brucye, Lorraine, Erik, Bice, Noah, and Ian.

To Diane, John, Mary, Winston, and Aldo.

And to Drs. Gordon Burghardt, A. Stanley Rand, and Dagmar I. Werner for their magnificent contributions to our understanding of the biology and welfare of iguanas.

THE LAZY IGUANA

by Fredric L. Frye

When asked to clean up his room,
"*I don't wanna*", said the iguana, "*it's not my place*".
Then help with the yard.
"*I don't wanna*", said the iguana, "*it's not my place*".
How about pitching in with the dishes?
"*I don't wanna*", said the iguana, "*it's not my place*".
Please take out the trash.
"*I don't wanna*", said the iguana, "*it's not my place*".
Will you help serve dinner?"
"*I don't wanna*", said the iguana, "*it's not my place*".
Well then, help watch for the DEADLY ANACONDA!
"*I don't wanna*", said the iguana, "*it's not my place*".
   Say, now, if you are not going to do
   ANYTHING to help, just what ARE you
   going to do?
"*I'm going to take a nice long nap; I really can't take the frantic pace*".

AT THIS TIME, ALONG CAME THE DEADLY ANACONDA, AND—
SNAP!!
HE FOUND THE IGUANA'S *PLACE!*

ACKNOWLEDGMENTS

The authors wish to express their gratitude to Robert E. Krieger, Marie Bowles, and the entire editorial and production staffs of the Krieger Publishing Co. for their enthusiastic and cheerful support of this project.

Brucye Frye graciously copy edited the early drafts of the manuscript for this book and made many thoughtful suggestions for making the book as "user-friendly" as possible to persons unfamiliar with veterinary medical terminology. Her efforts are much appreciated.

We are also grateful to veterinary colleagues and their iguana-owning clients for sharing some of their experiences with these fascinating creatures.

Books by Fredric L. Frye:

Husbandry, Medicine, and Surgery in Captive Reptiles
Biomedical and Surgical Aspects of Captive Reptile Husbandry
Phyllus, Phallus, Genghis Cohen and Other Creatures I Have Known
First Aid for Your Dog
First Aid for Your Cat
Schnauzers, a Complete Owner's Guide
Mutts, A Complete Owner's Guide; simultaneously published in the United
Kingdom as Mongrels, a Complete Owner's Guide
Biomedical and Surgical Aspects of Captive Reptiles, 2nd Ed., in two
volumes
A Practical Guide for Feeding Captive Reptiles
Captive Invertebrates: A Guide to Their Biology and Husbandry

INTRODUCTION

Lizards which resemble those living today have been around for many millions of years. Fossils of prehistoric lizards that lived 260 million years ago have been found. So when one considers that even then lizards had already existed for many millions of years, the true age for the dawning of these animals must date to well over 300 million years before the present time. These reptiles have been remarkably successful and have exploited many disparate habitats; presently they can be found on all continents except Antarctica, although in eons past, they lived there also when the land that was destined to become a continent was attached to the super landmass Gondwana and was a much warmer place.

Of the more than 3,000 species of lizards living today, some of the iguanas are the most popular reptiles kept in captivity as pets or study animals.

The common green iguana has, over the past twenty years, become an increasingly popular pet in North America and in parts of Europe and Asia. These large and impressively colored lizards often become docile, interact with their owners and, with proper care, may live for more than twenty years. Their daily needs for space, food, temperature maintenance, exercise, etc., are modest and can be easily satisfied if the owner knows what they are. Since iguanas can perceive red, orange, yellow, and green, this color vision can be used to advantage when inducing them to eat a nutritious home-prepared diet.

Iguanas are quiet and clean animals; thus, they are frequently kept as pets in apartments, condominiums, and townhouses when larger, noisier creatures would be forbidden by tenant membership rules. Some iguanine lizards are listed as threatened or endangered species and are protected under one or more international treaties. Consequently, they are not available in the pet trade.

Some of the larger iguanas, particularly the common green iguana, rock, and ground iguanas display an amazing intelligence; many learn to recognize their owners, and can be trained to use a cat litter-filled tray or other designated elimination area. With compassionate care, they usually become very tame and responsive to their owners, and, when obtained as hatchlings, a degree of human-animal bonding appears to take place. One particularly striking aspect of this behavior is discussed in the next to last chapter.

In this book, the authors provide information on how to properly care for iguanas and, where appropriate, have included anecdotes, personal experiences and even tales that may, at first glance, appear to be facetious. We wish to assure you that all of these stories are true—as anyone who has a long-term commitment or experience with these lizards can vouchsafe. This guide was not written to serve as a substitute for appropriate professional veterinary medical care when you have health problems with your iguana; however, it will help you avoid many of the common health-related difficulties that these lizards experience, and will characterize the important signs or symptoms of numerous diseases.

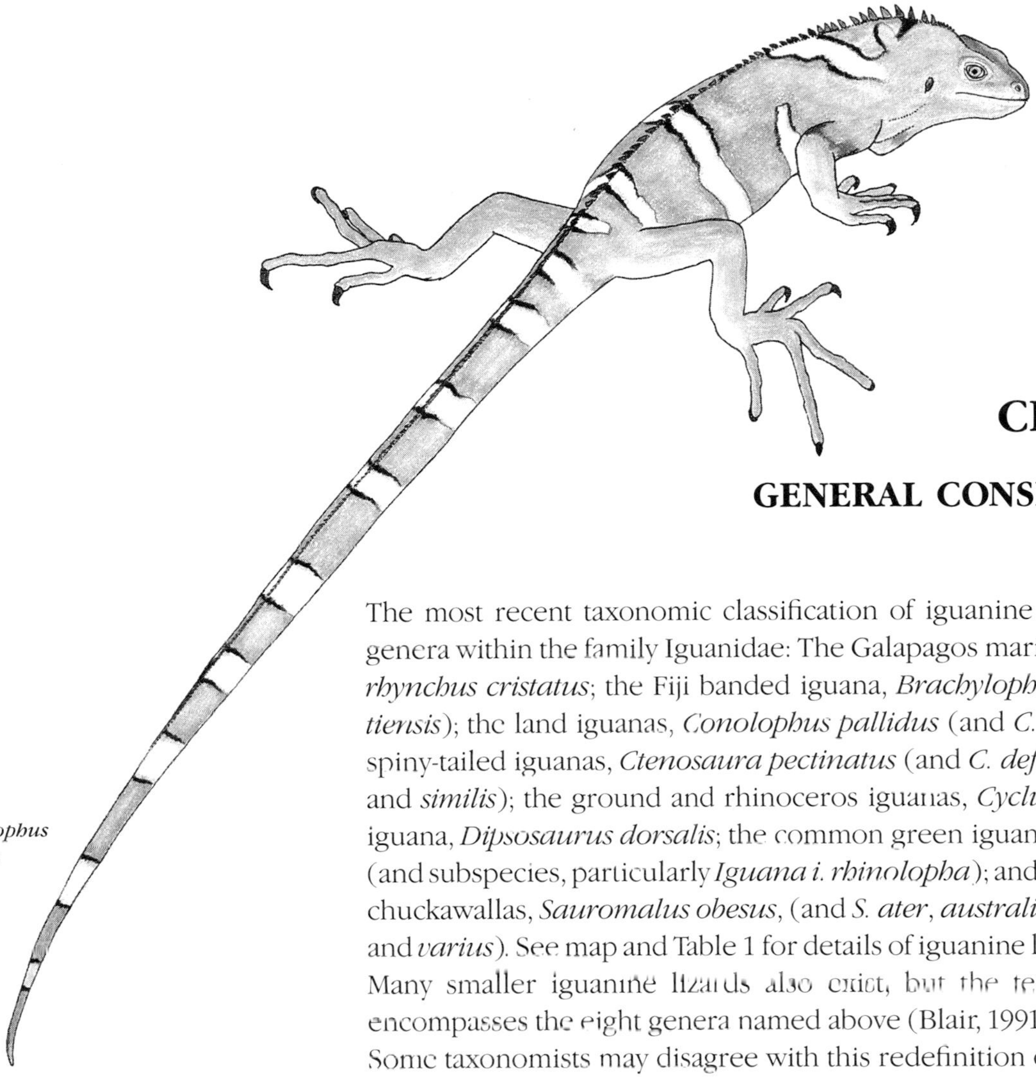

CHAPTER 1

GENERAL CONSIDERATIONS

Brachylophus vitiensis

The most recent taxonomic classification of iguanine lizards lists eight genera within the family Iguanidae: The Galapagos marine iguana, *Amblyrhynchus cristatus*; the Fiji banded iguana, *Brachylophus faciatus* (*B. vitiensis*); the land iguanas, *Conolophus pallidus* (and *C. subcristatus*); the spiny-tailed iguanas, *Ctenosaura pectinatus* (and *C. defensor, hemilopha,* and *similis*); the ground and rhinoceros iguanas, *Cyclura* sp.; the desert iguana, *Dipsosaurus dorsalis*; the common green iguana, *Iguana iguana* (and subspecies, particularly *Iguana i. rhinolopha*); and the rock-dwelling chuckawallas, *Sauromalus obesus*, (and *S. ater, australis, hispidus, slevini,* and *varius*). See map and Table 1 for details of iguanine lizard distribution. Many smaller iguanine lizards also exist, but the term "iguana" now encompasses the eight genera named above (Blair, 1991; Etheridge, 1982). Some taxonomists may disagree with this redefinition of the iguanas, but for this discussion, it serves us well. See Table 1 and Figure 1.

The common green iguana, *Iguana iguana*, and its closely related subspecies, *Iguana iguana rhinolopha*, are the ones which most commonly are kept as pets. The animals are very similar with the exception of the two or more small "horn"-like scales on the rostrum of the latter, which was first described as "*Lacerta iguana*" by Linaeus in his **SYSTEMA NATURAE** in 1758. One hundred and forty years later, the scientific nomenclature was augmented to include *Iguana (Hypsilophus) rhinolophus* as a subspecies from Veracruz, Mexico. These lizards have also been known as "*Iguana tuberculata*" Laurenti, described in 1768, and "*Iguana viridis*" Spix, described in 1825. *Iguana i. rhinolopha* has been found in several Central American sites as well as some islands within the Caribbean Sea (Etheridge, 1982; Köhler, 1991a).

The Latin American common green and spiny-tailed iguanas and the Fiji banded iguanas dwell in ecological communities consisting of rain

Figure 1. Global distribution of iguanine lizards. For illustration, males were chosen because of their more brilliant adult coloration. Illustration by W. Townsend, modified from Burghardt and Rand, 1982. See endsheets.

1

TABLE 1
Global Distribution of Iguanine Lizards

Common Name	Genus	Number of Species	Geographic Range
Marine Iguana	*Amblyrhynchus*	1	Galapagos Islands
Banded Iguanas} Crested Iguanas}	*Brachylophus*	2	Fiji and Tonga Islands
Land Iguanas	*Conolophus*	2	Galapagos Islands
Spiny-Tailed Iguanas	*Ctenosaura*	9	Mexico, Panama, and Colombian islands
Ground and Rock Iguanas	*Cyclura*	7	Caribbean islands
Desert Iguana	*Dipsosaurus*	1	Southwestern United States and Mexico; islands in the Gulf of Mexico
Green Iguanas	*Iguana*	2	Mexico to southern Brazil and Paraguay; Lesser Antilles
Chuckawallas	*Sauromalus*	6	Southwestern United States and Mexico; islands in the Gulf of Mexico

Modified from Etheridge, 1982.

forests, woodlands and sparsely wooded savannahs with rocky outcroppings. The distribution of these iguanas nearly a half-world apart further supports the role that plate tectonics plays in the dispersion of flora and fauna over the Earth's surface. The desert iguana and chuckawallas inhabit more xeric desert life zones; the chuckawallas prefer rocky masses with numerous cracks and crevices in which to take refuge from predators. The Galapagos ground iguanas live on the several islands in the Galapagos archipelago; and the other ground and rock iguanas are native to several islands throughout the Caribbean and Gulf of Mexico regions and on some of the eastern Central and South American shores. These lizards occupy several major ecological niches: rain forest, woodland, savannah, and desert terrestrial; arboreal; and marine aquatic, and have been remarkably successful in their exploitation of all of these diverse habitats.

Most of these lizards possess a dorsal crest of prominent dermal spines that courses along the midline from the neck to near the tail base; it is greatly reduced in the desert and spiny-tailed iguanas, and chuckawallas lack it entirely. Except for the chuckawallas and, to a lesser extent, the spiny-tailed and desert iguanas, most of these lizards are characterized by extendable dewlaps that serve several important purposes: for thermoregulation, they assist in heat absorption and radiation; and during courtship and combat rituals, they are displayed like a palette upon which sexually important colors are exhibited. The common green, Fiji, ground, and rock iguanas are laterally compressed; the desert iguanas are more cylindrical; and the chuckawallas and spiny-tailed iguanas are dorsoventrally compressed. In the chuckawallas and spiny-tailed lizards, this flattened shape enhances the habit of these creatures to seek refuge in fissures and crevices between large boulders where they inflate their large lungs thereby greatly increasing their body diameter, thus making it difficult to extract them from the cracks. This preference to seek refuge in cracks and crevices is termed *thigmotaxis*, and these lizards are said to be *thigmotactic*.

Figure 2—see page 85.

Iguanas possess a parietal or "third" eye on the dorsal midline of the skull, immediately behind the level of the two lateral eyes (Figure 2). Rather than being employed as a primary visual organ, this interesting sense organ serves as a dosimeter of radiant solar energy; it helps regulate the amount of time that these lizards spend exposed as they bask in direct sunlight. Also, it is intimately associated with the maturation of the sex organs and other endocrine glands, particularly the thyroid. The parietal eye probably only responds to shadows rather than transmitting discrete images to the brain; this ability could be of survival value by providing the lizard warning of attack by a predatory bird overhead.

Obvious sexual dimorphism or sex linked differences are present in some iguanas. The sex of even hatchlings often can be differentiated by someone experienced with these lizards. In some genera, the mature males are characterized by their robust body build, significantly larger head, neck, and jowls, more highly developed dorsal spinal crest, highly developed femoral pores (Figure 3), more vivid coloration during the mating season, and greater cross-sectional diameter of the tail base. Also, adult male green iguanas tend to possess a slightly shorter body than mature females of the same snout-to-vent length (SVL); in other genera, these differences in the sexes are more subtle. The reasons for these variations relate to the mating habits, and will be discussed briefly here and more fully later when reproduction is described. During bouts of ritual combat or courting that immediately precede copulation, males display their colors, extend their dewlaps, and go through much head-bobbing and high-stepping "body language." Chasing and biting of opponents are frequently observed. Objects within the home ranges of the combatants are rubbed with glandular secretions from the ventral portions of the thighs. During this mild abrasion, a waxy substance that is thought to contain a chemical cue, called a pheromone, is applied to branches, rocks, and receptive female lizards. This substance is produced by specialized structures, called femoral pores, mentioned earlier and serves to mark the territories and mates of successful or dominant male iguanas. The tail base of the males is larger because the twin copulatory organs, called *hemipenes*, are located in this site. Each hemipenis is connected to its respective right or left testicle by a vas deferens which is located within the body cavity. Females are more slightly built, with a narrower head and neck, greater length between the forelimbs and the hindlimbs, shorter and

FIGURE 3

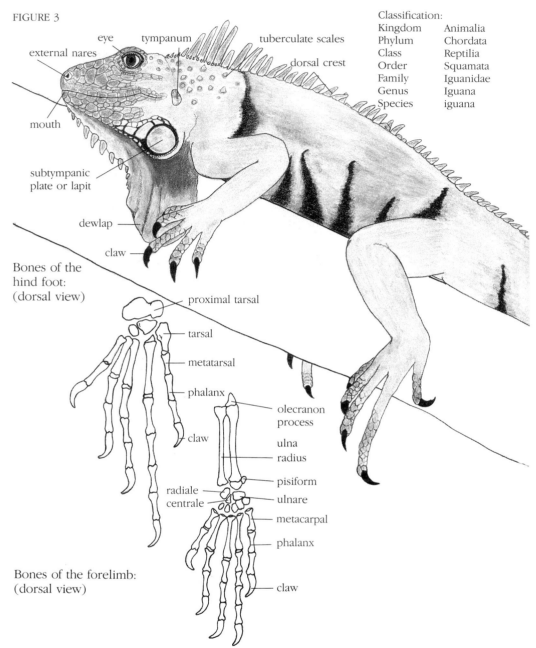

Classification:
Kingdom	Animalia
Phylum	Chordata
Class	Reptilia
Order	Squamata
Family	Iguanidae
Genus	Iguana
Species	iguana

Figure 3 a. Superficial external anatomy and fore- and hindlimb skeletal features of a green iguana. Illustration by W. Townsend.

4

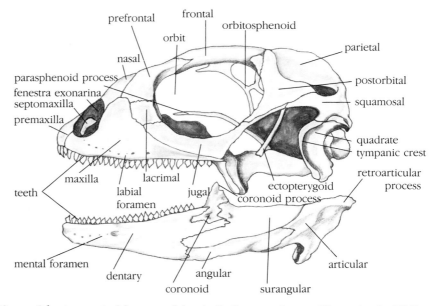

Figure 3 b. Anatomical features of the skull of a green iguana. Illustration by W. Townsend.

thinner dorsal spines, less robust neck and jowls and a slimmer round tail, and they retain the color that they had in their youth throughout much of their lives. Figures 3 a & 3 b illustrate some superficial features and the fore- and hindlimb appendages and skull features of a green iguana. Figure 4 illustrates the internal anatomy of a female green iguana.

As is the case with other scaly reptiles, iguanas periodically molt or "shed" their old worn out epidermis. Skin shedding is consistent with growth, occurring frequently with the rapid increase in size of young iguanas. Sloughing of the skin becomes less frequent as growth slows, but never ceases entirely.

All varieties of female iguanas are egg laying. After fertilization which occurs in the upper oviduct, the fertilized eggs receive their leathery eggshells as they pass down successive portions of the glandular oviduct. After selecting a suitable nesting site in sandy or humus-laden soil, the gravid females excavate a nest chamber in which they deposit their elongated eggs, and then cover them with the soil that was removed during the construction of the chamber. After depositing their eggs, the iguanas do not guard the nests, and more than one female may deposit her eggs in the same nesting site. Once the fertile eggs have been deposited and exposed to air, they begin their embryonic development; significant embryonic growth does not occur while the eggs are within the female iguana's body. The number of eggs deposited depends upon several criteria: the age and

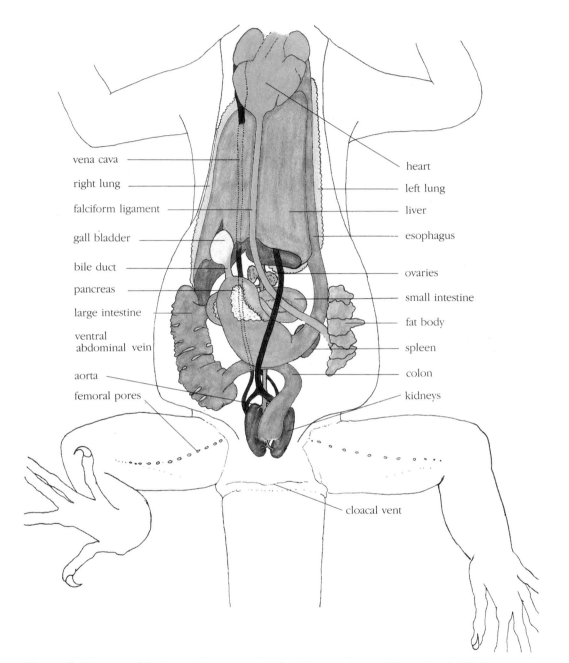

vena cava
right lung
falciform ligament
gall bladder
bile duct
pancreas
large intestine
ventral abdominal vein
aorta
femoral pores

heart
left lung
liver
esophagus
ovaries
small intestine
fat body
spleen
colon
kidneys

cloacal vent

Figure 4. Diagram of the internal anatomy of a female green iguana. Illustration by W. Townsend.

size of the female; her nutritional condition and health status; the fertility of the male; the taxonomic classification of the particular species, etc. Incubation time is largely dependent upon temperature. Each iguana genus has its own rather narrow range of incubation time, but these times usually last from a brief period of about five weeks to approximately three months. Hatchlings "pip," or slit, the pliant eggshells from which they emerge with a tooth-like "caruncle" on the snout that soon disappears. After slitting the egg, a hatchling may remain within the open confines of the shell for a period of a few hours to over a day (Figure 5). During this time, the balance of the yolk contained within the yolk sac is absorbed into the newly hatched lizard and the umbilicus closes to leave a slit-like scar on the ventral belly that, after a few sheds, disappears. The young iguana hatchlings are independent once they have exited the eggshell. After emerging from the eggshell, the infant iguanas begin to fend for themselves. Feeding usually does not commence immediately but, rather, a few days to a week or more passes before the little lizards begin to forage. During this time, the baby iguanas live on their residual stored yolk. Also, they acquire the important fermentative bacteria and protozoans largely responsible for digesting the cellulose-rich vegetable substances upon which they subsist. These bacteria and protozoa are actively ingested along with fresh feces of older iguanas (Troyer, 1982, 1984). It is essential that the digestive tracts of naïve, or newly hatched, lizards obtain these inoculating microorganisms.

Dietary preferences change substantially as the green, ground, and rhinoceros iguanas grow toward young adulthood. As youngsters, these iguanas eat significant amounts of animal-based food; when approximately half- to two-thirds grown, they begin to consume more and more vegetable matter. This change in diet coincides with the migration of the common green and Fiji banded iguanas from the ground, or near to the soil, into ever higher vegetation. Once they are fully grown, the majority of their food intake consists of leaves, tendrils, blossoms, and fruits. Being opportunistic, if they encounter eggs, nestling birds, small mammals, arachnids, caterpillars, and other invertebrates, they will eat them, but these items represent only a minor amount of the total diet. The change in diet makes sense when you understand that the requirement for protein diminishes markedly once growth slows. Sexual maturity occurs in the second or third year, depending upon whether the lizards grow to maturity in their native habitats or in captivity.

Today, a few successful breeding programs for the common green iguana, *Iguana iguana* (Banks, 1984 and others); the Fiji iguana, *Brachylophus faciatus* (Arnett, 1979); and several species of rhinoceros iguana, *Cyclura cornuta* (Tonge & Bloxam, 1984), *C. nubila* and *C.* sp. Duval (undated, cited by Tonge & Bloxam, 1984; Haast, 1969; Shaw, 1969; Burch-

Figure 5—see page 85.

field Roman, 1978; and Peters, 1982) have been reported throughout the world. Some of these breeding attempts were initiated to increase local populations of wild iguanas. Many native populations were severely depleted because of uncontrolled habitat loss, hunting pressure, and egg removal from nests. Conserving existing wild communities of iguanas in their natural habitats should be more easily accomplished than under even sophisticated artificial captive conditions. One goal for these breeding programs is to encourage the indigenous people to establish and maintain viable populations of iguanas that can be cropped periodically for their eggs, meat, and skins. In either case, sufficient numbers of unrelated lizards must be included so that genetic diversity can be maintained.

Some of these captive breeding programs have experienced positive results for the first few years and generations, but then discover that the quality of breeding animals and their progeny, if any, have rapidly decreased to the point where reproductive output ceases altogether. Once inbreeding is permitted, the "gene pool" becomes concentrated with a marked increase in the incidence of deleterious genetic traits. Soon there is decrease in vigor. In his paper on captive breeding of the common green iguana at the Royal Melbourne Zoo in Australia, Banks (1984) suggested that the detrimental effects of inbreeding successive generations originating from a single pair of iguanas that may have been siblings were surprisingly swift and serious. The incidence of infertility, egg-hatching failure, embryonic and fetal developmental abnormalities, and other problems rose in a directly parallel fashion with the coefficient of inbreeding. These experiences confirm the absolute necessity for genetic diversity when attempting to breed these lizards in captivity or under wild conditions.

BASIC BEHAVIOR OF GREEN (and some other) IGUANAS

Aspects of green iguana behavior are found throughout this text and are not confined to a single chapter. This section, in a glossary format, is included as a quick reference to characterize some of the basic behavioral actions the captive iguana is observed to "do" on a somewhat regular basis. Some behavior is associated only with mature lizards. Generally, isolated iguanas exhibit certain behavior to a lesser degree than those kept in pairs or groups.

Closing of one or both eyes. While basking, iguanas may alternate closing one eye, keeping watch with the other. Eye closing, in addition to being a protective measure, is a response to both displays by other iguanas and to human touch. Submission, toleration or fear may be indicated.

Eye "bulging" or protrusion. Now and then, iguanas push their eyes out under closed lids for a few moments, and then rub them on a branch or similar surface. Presumably, this is to remove pieces of shedding skin, or to scratch an itch.

Sleeping. Iguanas go to sleep when the sun goes down, closing both eyes and extending their limbs back against their bodies in a relaxed position. They awake at sunrise, and do not enjoy being disturbed or handled during the night.

Tongue-testing (or flicking) and licking. Tongue-testing is comparable to sniffing, having a sensory function. Iguanas explore new or unfamiliar things in their environment by lightly touching them with their tongues. They also frequently reaffirm familiar objects, food, human hands, and particularly other iguanas by tongue-testing. Iguanas clean their teeth and lips by both licking and wiping them on branches or other surfaces.

Cautious exploratory behavior. This behavior is associated with the passage of what the iguana perceives to be a potential threat. The lizard will creep along, evaluating his surroundings by visual scanning and much tongue-testing. Similar behavior is exhibited by the subadult female iguana when entering a territory which may be occupied by an adult male iguana, and is perhaps both cautious and submissive.

Opening the mouth. This is usually part of a defensive or aggressive display, often accompanied by expulsion of air in a hiss, primarily but not exclusively, to warn other iguanas. When overheated or exerted, iguanas will pant. (If a confined iguana is seen panting, his living arrangements may not be permitting a temperature gradient. Adjustments must be made, as overheating is dangerous for an iguana.) Iguanas also yawn, opening the mouth widely and then shutting it abruptly. This is entirely normal behavior.

Head-bobbing. Head-bobbing is a major means of communication, and is intended primarily but not exclusively for other iguanas. The head is tossed upward and brought down in sequence varying in degree and number, depending on the nature of the display. Head-bobbing is generally associated with territoriality and assertion of dominance. Both male and female lizards bob, the former more often and with greater exaggeration and variation. Isolated iguanas will head-bob, but less frequently than those kept in pairs or groups. Other head movements, such as shaking, are associated with courtship or irritants. Many iguanas will respond to their owner's head-bobbing by vigorously "answering" with their own.

Dewlap extension and retraction. The dewlap is extended to increase surface area for heat and light absorption. During territorial displays or if threatened, the iguana will extend his dewlap to give the head an imposing appearance. Because the dewlap of male iguanas is more highly developed than that of the female, these displays are far more impressive in adult males. The iguana retracts his dewlap to minimize appearance, in an attempt to become obscure to a potential attacker or predator (Figure 6).

Figure 6—see p. 85.

Lateral body flattening. Not to be confused with inflation of the body (as when captured), lateral flattening, usually accompanied by raising the dorsal crest and dewlap extension, gives the iguana a larger appearance and is both a combative and defensive display.

Tail twitchings and lashing. A fight between mature male iguanas includes initial twitching of the tail with intermittent lashes. Nervous iguanas are observed to twitch the tips of their tails. Frightened or cornered lizards strike out pointedly with defensive lashes.

Color changes. An iguana's color can change within minutes and occurs in response to temperature fluctuation, physical condition and social status. At the onset of basking, the iguana's overall color darkens and lateral bands become prominent. As the lizard's body temperature increases to high levels, coloration lightens, with the head becoming white in extreme heat. Chilled, sick, injured, depressed or defeated iguanas are darker while active; dominant lizards have a lightened color. Many female green iguanas retain their green color when mature (Figure 7 a), whereas most color changes related to social status are associated with mature males. Six or eight weeks prior to and during courtship, male iguanas acquire bright gold or orange coloring over much of the body, as well as a whitened head (Figure 7 b). Lone males may exhibit this coloration more subtly.

Everting hemipenes. Mature male iguanas are observed to evert both hemipenes partially or entirely, discharging a moist, whitish, substance which may have shreds of partially dried material mixed with it. With some males, this occurs almost daily; others will pass this secretion seasonally, or as a prelude to, or during, courtship.

Skin shedding. Shedding is consistent with growth, occurring frequently with the rapid size increase of young iguanas. Sloughing of the old epidermis becomes less frequent as growth slows, but never stops completely.

Escape, defense, and fearful behavior. An iguana will flatten his body and shrink behind a branch or other cover and remain motionless, becoming obscure to a potential threat. If caught, escape efforts include freezing up and/or rotating and writhing. Similar behavior is discussed within the **RESTRAINT** section of this text.

Bodily "jolt". Healthy, contented iguanas are occasionally observed to make this seemingly involuntary movement consisting of a brief, strong twitch while sitting upright. It is apparently no cause for concern.

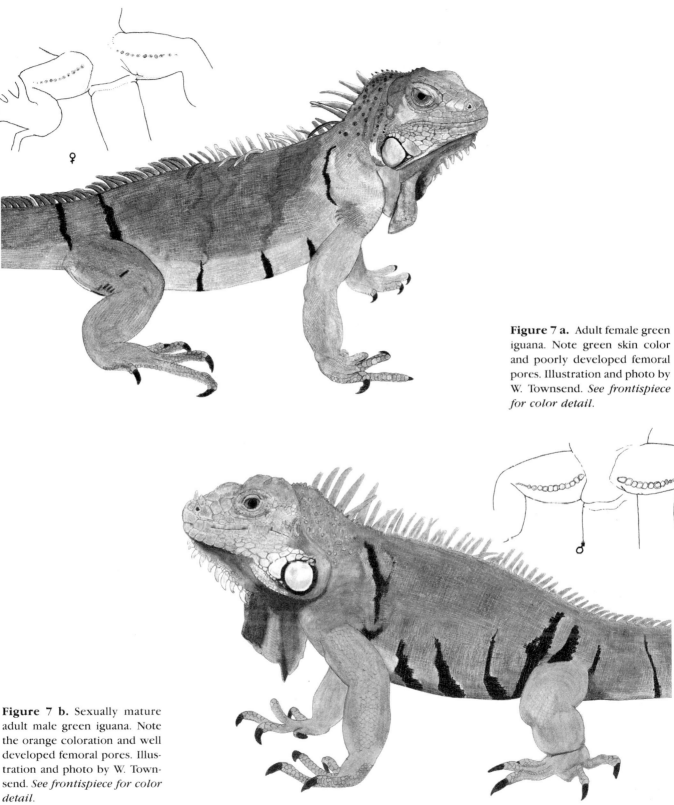

Figure 7 a. Adult female green iguana. Note green skin color and poorly developed femoral pores. Illustration and photo by W. Townsend. *See frontispiece for color detail*.

a

Figure 7 b. Sexually mature adult male green iguana. Note the orange coloration and well developed femoral pores. Illustration and photo by W. Townsend. *See frontispiece for color detail*.

b

Geophagy and lithophagy. As iguanas move along the ground tongue-testing various surfaces, they sometimes nibble on or eat dust, sand, rocks, debris, or other foreign matter.

Sneezing. It is entirely normal for iguanas to sneeze frequently. These lizards possess glands in their nasal cavities which secrete concentrated salt solution which is expelled through this sneezing activity. This behavior is discussed at greater detail in the **NUTRITION** section of this book.

Territorial behavior. Territoriality is innate in iguanas and serves to preserve each species in its most vigorous state. Because territoriality is innate, the iguana keeper should be familiar with this behavior, as it is exhibited by captive lizards as well as wild ones.

There is infrequent competition for food, as this would be energetically wasteful and generally unnecessary, particularly for herbivores. Of primary concern to iguanas, both captive and wild, are available perches and basking areas, both for basking and male displaying. Optimum digestion occurs at higher temperatures and enables peak utilization of nutrients, promoting faster growth and superior fitness. In turn, the larger, healthier lizard has a higher likelihood for survival, with the fittest male securing choice mating territory and enough females to ensure his contribution to the genetic pool.

Cannibalism. Although it would seem totally counterproductive to the survival of a species for it to engage in feeding upon its young, some iguanas, particularly the spiny-tailed iguana, *Ctenosaura similis* do so, and instances have been well documented (Fitch and Henderson, 1978; Mitchell, 1986; Mora, 1991). Interestingly, this behavior is not necessarily induced by the artificiality of captivity, but has been found to occur in wild populations of lizards. It has been suggested that cannibalism offers several advantages. For instance, it eliminates potential competitors and it benefits some members of a population during times of food scarcity when the young would find it difficult to survive (Mora, 1991).

Pacing. Sometimes, an iguana displays signs of its rejection of captivity by constant pacing along the edges of its cage, digging into the substrate, or rubbing its nose on the walls or boundaries of its enclosure. If a lizard persists in any of these behaviors, it is likely that something within its immediate captive environment is either lacking or distressing. Recommendations for accommodating an iguana that paces are given in the housing chapter. For additional information on the rich behavioral repertoire of iguanine lizards, the reader is referred to Auffenberg, 1982; Carpenter, 1982; Distel, 1982; Drummond and Burghardt, 1982; Gibbons and Watkins, 1982; Dugan, 1982; Dugan and Wiewandt, 1982; Ryan, 1982; and Werner, 1982.

SELECTING AN IGUANA

The most often asked question regarding the acquisition of a new iguana probably is whether to purchase a hatchling or a well-started juvenile or adult. Today, with increasing numbers of captive-bred youngsters, it is possible to select a healthy, unparasitized, and "head-started" lizard of about 1–3 months of age. By this age, the baby iguana should be eating well and already growing vigorously.

When shopping for a first iguana pet, the prospective owner is often faced with choosing from a tank containing anywhere from 5 to 35 little green lizards. Physical clues to a healthy choice are (1) well-rounded, fleshy hind limbs and tail, and (2) green, lustrous skin. Protruding pelvic bones and yellow-green and wrinkled skin are signs that the lizard is not in optimum condition. Behavioral traits which indicate good health include alertness and an upright posture, as opposed to sleepiness or lethargy. If the iguana is eating or is reasonably active, is exploring its boundaries by tongue-flicking here and there, and is not hyperactive or fearful, it is a good choice.

There is nothing inherently wrong with obtaining an iguana as an adult as long as it is healthy and parasite free. However, many, if not most, of the adult iguanas available from reptile dealers are wild-caught animals who have survived the trauma of being captured, held in enclosures that are likely to be less than hygienic, and grouped with other lizards that have not been segregated by size, sex, territorial dominance, or health. They may not have been fed nor received fresh water for several weeks. Consequently, many wild-caught iguanas arrive at their final destination at a pet dealer's establishment burdened by intestinal and/or external parasites, malaria, abscesses, and malnutrition. When large numbers are housed together, they crawl over one another and their sharp claws, which are often covered with feces, may penetrate the skin of others and, in doing so, cause infections. Adult iguanas can sometimes be obtained from owners that no longer can keep them; adopting one of these "domesticated" lizards has several advantages. usually they are healthier than newly arrived wild-caught animals, and since they have adapted to the conditions of captivity, they are used to being handled.

As soon as possible, the feces of the newly acquired iguana should be examined microscopically for the presence of harmful parasites. Most veterinarians provide this service at a modest fee. This analysis is particularly important for iguanas whose previous living conditions are questionable or who are to be introduced to one or more resident lizards in a collection.

On the other hand, excepting a clearly serious disorder, adopting the physically imperfect iguana should not be disregarded. Many "damaged" iguanas can be rehabilitated and make lovely pets. Usually, "rehabilitated" simply means providing the iguana with good care, and perhaps a visit to a veterinarian who is competent with reptiles. Imperfect lizards are periodically obtained through classified ads, adoption committees of local herpetological society chapters, and the herpetological "grapevine." Several stories of particular adopted "damaged" iguanas are included later in this text; see Chapter 9, **WENDY'S OBSERVATIONS**.

The major things to look for are: bright eyes; no discharges from eyes or nose; the absence of lumps, bumps, or discolored patches of skin; no malformed or missing digits; and no fecal or urinary staining on the belly or tail.

A routine microscopic examination of a newly acquired iguana's feces is recommended because this fecal examination is the best means for determining whether or not an iguana is free of harmful parasites. Many veterinarians provide this service which is inexpensive, and is especially crucial if a newly acquired iguana, whose previous living conditions are questionable, is to be introduced to one or more iguanas. It is wise to have any new (wild-caught) iguana's blood examined for the presence of malarial parasites also. This test which is inexpensive and requires taking only a minute quantity of blood from the lizard's tail vein can be performed by a veterinarian whose practice includes reptiles.

HANDLING

The quality of the rapport between the pet iguana and the keeper depends upon:
• The psychological environment, specifically privacy; the provision of a hiding box.
• The keeper's understanding of the iguana's nature. Refer to the **BEHAVIOR** section of this book.
• The type and frequency of interaction between the keeper and the lizard.

The relationship you have with your iguana will be based on, in addition to good husbandry, your physical presence, i.e., whether or not your movements are intimidating, and the way you handle and touch your pet.

Excepting physical contact during basking, mating and territorial disputes, mutual touching is not noted to be a large part of the iguana's usual communications. It stands to reason, then, that for the captive iguana the human touch may be perceived as anything from an attack to a minor annoyance. Still, it is apparent that once tame, pet iguanas like being gently stroked on some areas; therefore, between you and your iguana, touch is a major means of communication. Teach your pet to associate human hands not only with feeding, but also with the pleasant sensation of being caressed. You can convey kindness and reassurance of your familiarity through your touch. This is easily done! Realize that the pet iguana is sentient, can experience fear, and is aware of his captivity. CARE for your pet and the right touch will follow naturally. Once an iguana is accustomed to interaction with people, the question, "How much handling is too much?" is determined by the lizard's behavior. Generally, tame iguanas can be handled frequently (if done considerately) as long as the iguana is healthy, is at ease, and is feeding regularly.

Lifting and Carrying

Figure 3 a—see page 4.

When picking up a green iguana, it is helpful to understand the arboreal adaptions of the lizard. In nature, green iguanas are most secure at heights, usually resting on the elevated branches of a tree. The lengthy digits of the rear limbs and the claws are ideal for climbing (Figure 3 a). Each claw can be described as having a "lock-release" mechanism. When iguanas descend a tree trunk or branch, they ease themselves down by alternately locking in and releasing the claws. Even the very slightly prehensile tail presses against the tree for stability, and does not hang uselessly (Figure 8 a). If the iguana becomes insecure in its position or feels threatened, it will tighten its grip on a surface (including your hand or arm) by digging in with its claws. This is important to remember when approaching an iguana, especially a hatchling. The limbs and toes of a baby iguana are particularly fragile, and care must be taken when lifting a small lizard from the branch, clothing, upholstery, or other surface to which it is clinging.

Ease a finger under each hand or foot to disengage the claws from the surface while keeping the other hand in front of the lizard's head. Iguanas do not like to be grabbed around the neck or midsection from above (Figure 8 b).

Be a passive handler. Allow your iguana to climb onto you by easing your hand anteriorly under the forelimbs (Figure 8 c).

If your iguana turns away or tries to avoid you, persist with patience. Gently corner the iguana, making it necessary for it to climb onto you. At this point, if your pet is nervous and jumpy, you will need to hold onto it. Never grab an iguana, large or small, tame or wild, by the tail. The idea is to let the iguana feel it is being supported rather than caught (Figure 8 d).

If an iguana feels caught, it will usually writhe and wriggle in an attempt to get free. In this case, do not drop the lizard. Maintain a firm but

15

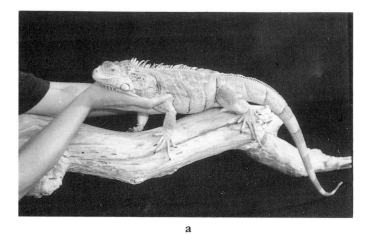

a

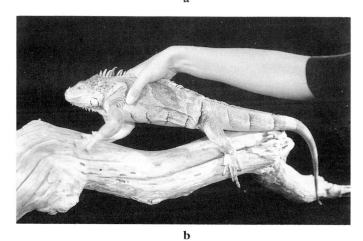

b

c

d

e

Figure 8. Sequence of photographs illustrating handling and restraint of an iguana. Note how lizard grasps branch when picked up from above. Photos by W. Townsend.

gentle hold on the thoracic and pelvic regions with the limbs pinioned, as described in **RESTRAINT**, until the lizard becomes calm (Figure 8 e).

Once the iguana is at ease, slowly release your hold and encourage the lizard to climb from one hand to the other, or to sit on your shoulder. Your shoulder is an attractive place to an iguana. The top of your head is even better. To discourage the iguana from climbing on your face to get to the top of your head (which he will eventually try to do), place your hand between the iguana's face and yours.

Biting

Iguanas have many small, sharp teeth lining the upper and lower jaws. A large iguana is capable of giving a painful, damaging bite—but then, so is a cat or a dog.

Green iguanas are generally nonaggressive. Unless you have a wild-caught or untamed lizard, you are unlikely to be bitten. A newly acquired young iguana may try to bite defensively or when hungry, and some iguanas can be provoked into biting if persistently annoyed. Mature male iguanas are sometimes observed to bite on objects, including other iguanas and human hands that recently have been in contact with either a mature receptive female or another mature male iguana. Such behavior is probably caused by the presence of pheromones generally associated with sexual activity. It is prudent to wash your hands thoroughly between handlings of different adult iguanas.

For the most part, bite attempts are both predictable and avoidable. If you are ever bitten by a pet iguana, it will be because you threatened or angered him.

During a visit with a veterinarian, the following tale was related to the junior author. The client brought a very large pet iguana into the veterinarian's office and proceeded to kiss the lizard about the neck and head, and was subsequently severely bitten on the lips. Whether or not this iguana was used to being kissed, it is likely that the stress of being taken out of the home, as well as whatever illness the lizard was suffering from, left him more than unreceptive to kissing. Some people who become fond of their iguanas inevitably feel the need to bestow a few kisses on their pets, and this is certainly understandable. However, keep in mind that such an expression of affection is likely to be perceived as an attack by an iguana either unaccustomed to such contact or under duress.

Some iguana keepers enthusiastically smother their tiny new pets with kisses. The lizards usually close both eyes and become motionless, probably waiting to be eaten. In time, these iguanas get used to this and lose their fear of being close to the human face. We recommend a more gradual approach to familiarizing your pet with yourself via speaking softly, handling gently and regularly, and hand feeding. Reserve kisses for thoroughly tame iguanas—or for other humans.

Hand feeding

Hand feeding is an excellent way to hasten acclimation. When your iguana accepts food from your hand, a rewarding, mutually satisfying association occurs. Hand-fed lizards come to expect such treatment, and will not feed as heartily when simply left with a meal, no matter how appetizing (Figure 9 a & b).

Figure 9 a—see page 85.
Figure 9 b—see page 86.

"Difficult" Iguanas

Difficult iguanas are those that have been mishandled, deeply traumatized, or taken from the wild as adults. Such lizards may never become good pets, but as captives, deserve proper care nevertheless. Most prospective iguana keepers will want to avoid acquiring difficult iguanas which are characterized by a defensive or fearful response to human presence. Still, there are some people who feel compassion for mistreated or unfortunate living things, no matter how wretched they may seem to others, and feel challenged to "rehabilitate" or to provide a kind environment for such animals. A description of observed behavior as well as a few handling suggestions may prove useful to those who have taken in "difficult" iguanas.

Iguanas possess individual personalities, some becoming more sociable towards people than others. For the difficult iguana, trust of human hands was never established, perhaps due to insufficient or improper contact. A positive association with touching failed to occur, and possibly a negative association did. The iguana that flees headlong, crashing into the walls of his enclosure, is terrified. Hiding boxes are particularly crucial for such lizards. When picked up, the frightened iguana typically goes through several behavioral postures. After writhing or spinning in an attempt to escape, the lizard will "freeze," becoming pliant and motionless. Wide, unblinking eyes, a retracted dewlap, and an absence of tongue-flicking are noted. Nervous twitching of the tail may be the only movement. An iguana often breaks the immobility with a frantic escape attempt, lunging away from the handler. When this fails, the lizard becomes defensive, extending his dewlap, puffing up the body by inhalation, and expelling the air in a hiss. Tail-lashing and bite attempts may accompany this defensive behavior. When holding the difficult iguana, gently but firmly become like a somewhat confining branch, letting the lizard feel supported rather than caught. The handler can try to calm the iguana by stroking the dewlap area. While being careful of bite attempts, encourage the lizard to tongue-flick a finger. Hopefully, an association between human scent and a nonharmful, pleasant touch may form. This sort of handling session is recommended at the keeper's convenience, but should be somewhat regular, not excessive, and not within an hour of the lizard's mealtime. Try, for example, two 10-minute sessions daily for two or three weeks. (This is also a good handling schedule for newly acquired iguanas.)

At feeding time, do not *capture* the iguana, but do try to hand feed. Hold a little of the food between the dish and the lizard. Move closer to the lizard with the food, and wait a minute. If the iguana won't accept the offer, or flees, put the food down and slowly withdraw your hand. Back away from the enclosure until the iguana feeds. You may have to leave the room.

RESTRAINT

Rock and ground rhinoceros and the common green iguanas bear sharp claws on each of their digits, and they possess powerful tails with which they can flail predators and anyone who handles these lizards carelessly. Their claws can inflict severe lacerations on the arms of the unwary person. These lizards often become accustomed to being handled and are tolerant of manipulation, but it is important to know the proper manner for restraining these powerful lizards so that neither they nor their human handler is injured.

Generally, it is the claws and tail that are employed in defense. Therefore, the four limbs must be held against the lizard's body in such a way that the feet cannot be used in defense. If the lizard is clinging to a screen or wire mesh surface, carefully disengage its claws before lifting the animal; if it is merely plucked from the screen, its nails may be torn out or its toes may sustain fractures. It is extremely important when grasping the limbs not to exert excessive force on the lower portion of the limbs, i.e., the hands or feet, because it is relatively easy to cause fractures of the upper segments, the arms or thighs, respectively. All that is necessary is to pinion the limbs against the body wall (Figure 10). If required, the limbs can be strapped against the body wall with cloth or gauze or, alternatively, the entire lizard can be confined to a length of stockinette or even a toeless cotton sock. Sticky adhesive, masking, duct, or transparent tapes should not be used because the adhesive removes the superficial epidermis where it is in contact with the skin.

Another means for short-time restraint has been described by the senior author (Frye, 1973, 1981, 1991a). This method relies upon a nervous response, called the *vago-vagal* effect, which slows the lizard's heart rate,

Figure 10. The limbs of this iguana are held firmly so that it cannot struggle free; however, the legs are not folded over its spine which could result in limb fractures. Photo by W. Townsend.

lowers its blood pressure, and induces short-term nonchemical torpor. It is safe and effective, but this technique should not be employed by inexperienced persons because, if applied incorrectly, delicate structures could be injured.

HOUSING

Ideal housing arrangements for a captive iguana have a ground area where the iguana can eat, drink and toilet; a sturdy branch or similar structure upon which the lizard can climb and bask; light/temperature control; and a hiding box for privacy. With these basic needs in mind, a variety of housing setups can be made.

Large dog houses or similar shelters can be used to provide additional shade as well as privacy. The size and conformation of accommodations for keeping captive iguanas depend largely upon (1) the kind of iguanas to be housed together; (2) the size of the individual animal at present and the size that it will attain at maturity; (3) the sex of the animal; and (4) the number of lizards that will be sharing the cage or enclosure. Other factors that should be considered are (1) whether the enclosure will be an indoors or outdoors structure; and (2) the climatic conditions to which the iguana will be exposed throughout the year.

All of the lizards discussed in this book prefer either tropical rain forest, relatively humid tropical or semitropical island, or desert ecological habitats. They will not tolerate being chilled, nor will they survive overheating. Therefore, if the day- or night-time temperatures are expected to drop below 23.3° C (74° F), any outdoor enclosure should be provided with supplementary heating in the form of radiant or other form of warmth; heating pads; subsurface solar or other circulated warm-water heating coils; overhead infrared heat lamps, etc. A roughly two-foot square area warmed by either a 100-watt standard bulb, a 75-watt red spot bulb, or a subsurface heating pad supports two adult iguanas.

In very warm climates, shade must be afforded these animals to prevent heat stress. This shade can be provided easily by one or more broad-leaf trees such as mulberry, *Morus* sp., whose leaves and fruit are edible and nutritious for iguanas. *Hibiscus* is another excellent choice for furnishing both adequate shade and edible leaves, flowers, and okra-like fruit pods.

It is important that a visual barrier be included at the periphery of the cage or enclosure in order to prevent the lizard from striking and/or rubbing its nose as it paces or explores its captive surroundings. If an iguana persists in digging or nose-rubbing, it is likely that something within its enclosure is either lacking or distressing. Insufficient hiding or refuge areas, intimidation by a cage mate, or even something within the lizard's view may cause anxiety. Careful observation and experimentation with housing adjustments are likely to resolve the problem and help the restless iguana to adjust to captivity and relax.

Male iguanas usually do not recognize the sex of juvenile iguanas, and will attack even hatchlings regardless of their sex. Therefore, mature male iguanas should not be housed together with smaller iguanas of either sex, unless it has been determined that the smaller female has been recognized *and accepted* by the males.

Generally, iguanas should not be kept in the same enclosure with other animals, particularly birds and other reptile species because of the possibility of transferring pathogenic bacteria or protozoa between these animals. Also, interspecies intimidation or even predation can occur when various animals of different species, classes, or body sizes are mixed. Lastly, combining different species usually complicates the task of maintaining cage hygiene.

As examples of noninstitutional environments, we offer the following diagrams (see Figure 11 a–c):

• A 4-foot Vitalite fixture hangs over the dog house, roughly 3 feet above the lizards that are basking. Vitalites are as close to the lizards as possible, but are not within their reach.

• Two red spotlights, one 75 watts, the other 250 watts, are suspended from plant hooks secured in the ceiling. These bulbs hang approximately 39 inches (1 meter) and 52 inches (1.3 meters), respectively, above the dog house. The juxtaposition of the full-spectrum fluorescent and heat bulbs allows for the desired illumination and warmth, but does not pose either a thermal burn or fire hazard.

• On warm days, the window is kept open, and the iguanas receive about an hour of unfiltered sunshine.

• A 2-foot full-spectrum fluorescent fixture hangs inside the dog house, and a radiant heating pad on a low setting is on the floor. The pad is covered by a large piece of artificial turf to prevent thermal burns. When used with a terrarium or other small cage, these electrical heating pads should be placed *beneath* the cage bottom, rather than inside the cage. Automatic light timers are ideal for controlling incandescent lighting and photoperiod.

• A standard 100-watt light bulb in a reflector fixture and a 2-foot Vitalite rest on the screen of a 55-gallon (approx. 220 liter) tank in the closet.

• One part of another heating pad on a low setting is underneath the large tank, and the other part is under a portion of a 7-gallon tank, which houses a hatchling iguana.

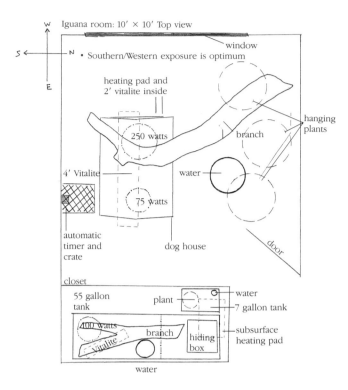

Iguana room: 10' × 10' Top view

window

• Southern/Western exposure is optimum

heating pad and 2' vitalite inside

250 watts

4' Vitalite

75 watts

automatic timer and crate

water

branch

hanging plants

dog house

door

closet

55 gallon tank

plant

water

7 gallon tank

100 watts

Vitalite

branch

hiding box

subsurface heating pad

water

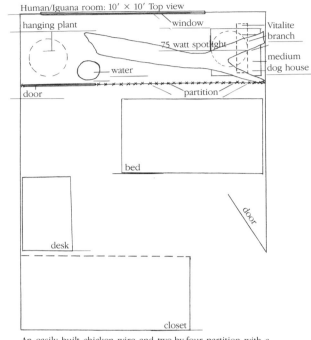

Human/Iguana room: 10' × 10' Top view

hanging plant

window

Vitalite branch

75 watt spotlight

water

medium dog house

door

partition

bed

desk

closet

door

An easily built chicken wire and two-by-four partition with a walk-in door designates the iguana area. The floor of the lizard's area can be covered with artificial turf and newspapers.

Shows the same dimensions as iguana room on left. A relatively small room but up to 3 large iguanas and one person can share the space comfortably. This is a great arrangement for a child—to share his or her room with such fascinating pets!

Human/Iguana room: front view. Lighting cords are affixed to first the ceiling and then the wall after being pushed through the screening.

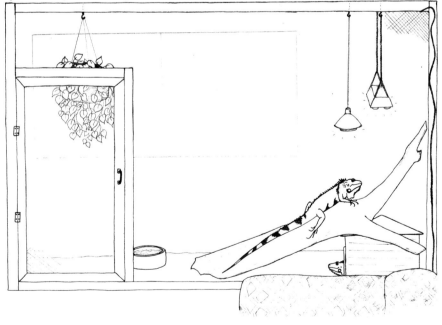

Figure 11. Diagrams of noninstitutional captive environments designed by the junior author. Illustrations by W. Townsend.

22

- All incandescent lights and heating pads are on an automatic timer which is enclosed by a plastic milk crate kept against the wall by the dog house, and plastic safety plugs are inserted or taped over unused wall sockets.
- The roof of the dog house and the floor are covered with artificial turf. There are both a large water bowl and a few newspapered toilet areas.
- A 9-foot (2.7 meter) long, 8-inch (20 cm) thick branch rests partly on the floor and partly on the dog house.
- Three giant pothos* plants hang from the ceiling and are misted periodically, as are the lizards. Another small pothos plant is in the 7-gallon (approx. 28 liter) tank for the hatchling.

Four large iguanas, one male and three females, share the room. They alternate using the inside of the dog house as they please. Three smaller iguanas, two females and one male, live within the 55-gallon (approx. 220 liters) tank, protected from the largest male.

The hatchling is taken outside at least every other day for no less than 15 minutes of sunshine, as no Vitalite is set up for his tank. Periodically, the lizards in the large tank also go out for some sunshine.

Though the lizards in the closet and the room are all aware of each other, the closet doors provide a visual barrier, and so minimize stress due to territorial activity. Eventually, the two smaller females will be recognized by the male and will be allowed to occupy the room. The small male will neither grow significantly bigger, nor be tolerated by the larger male. This little male's name is Peanut, and his story is included in the last chapter. Peanut is frequently given free range of the apartment as a break from his limited quarters.

The red spot lights are sometimes moved to warm different perches that are set up, depending upon the season and changes in the iguanas' social behavior and needs. A large, covered cat box full of damp sand and sphagnum moss is available for gravid females to excavate their nests.

Alternatively, indoor housing can be arranged by using an existing room and modifying it for sheltering one or several adult iguanas. Smaller single lizards can be kept in terraria until they outgrow their quarters.

As the male lizards mature and develop their territorial hierarchies, they become quite aggressive to any other lizards of their species, even hatchlings, which they have been known to attack and eat. Therefore, mature males should not be housed with other smaller iguanas of either sex unless it has been determined that any smaller females are recognized and accepted by the male. Most females are tolerant of each other, but may

---

*Although pothos is a mildly noxious plant like its *Philodendron* cousins, iguanas soon learn not to eat its leaves.

23

display aggression at the time that they deposit their eggs if adequate nesting material and space are not provided.

Water

Whatever the accommodations are, there must be provision for adequate fresh water at all times. Much of the iguana's metabolic requirement for water is obtained from the moisture contained in the leafy vegetation and soft fruits upon which it subsists, but it also will drink considerable volumes of fresh water. It is not an iguana's nature to drink from standing vessels of water; rather, it is accustomed to imbibing drops of rain water or condensed mist from leaves in its immediate environment. However, some captive iguanas will learn to drink from water dishes. This will be discussed in greater detail later in this chapter.

Ideally, larger enclosures should be fitted with a drainage system so that thorough cleansing of the cage can be facilitated. The inner surfaces of the cage should be treated to make them impervious to water; this treatment should be nontoxic, and the entire enclosure should be completely aired so that any noxious fumes or vapors are permitted to "outgas" and escape. Even raw plywood or pressed board materials should be allowed to outgas for several days to a week or more to allow any volatile adhesives to escape into the atmosphere.

Cages should be fitted with suitable entrance doors to permit access to the inhabitants and the interior of the enclosures. Tall cages should have more than one door so that all portions of the cage are accessible (see Figure 11).

Photoperiod

All lighting fixtures must be installed so that the iguanas cannot come into direct contact with them and so that water cannot be accidentally splashed on hot surfaces. All electrical wiring must be well insulated and installed according to existing building codes. Because they are native to near equatorial latitudes, most iguanas and their immediate lizard cousins require a photoperiod (a light:dark cycle) of approximately 12–14 hours of light daily. This is now recognized as an important factor in maintaining these animals in health and enhancing the likelihood of captive breeding; keeping these creatures in a regime of 24-hour light intensity is harmful, and will lead to declining health and will inhibit reproduction. Automatic light timers are ideal for conveniently maintaining an established photoperiod, and are inexpensive and readily available at hardware stores. As noted previously, some timers are designed for incandescent lights but are not suitable for fluorescent fixtures.

Ventilation

Although most of the iguanas listed earlier in this text originate from relatively humid habitats, artificial habitats must afford adequate air circulation so that the interiors of the cages never become overly moist and fetid. A few small screened holes at the lower portion of the cage and a few more at the top of the enclosure will permit a natural upward air flow that will carry surplus moisture upward and out from the cage. Large enclosures can employ appropriate exhaust fans to handle the necessary air flow.

The diagram and description of the iguana enclosure at San Diego Zoological Park exemplifies an excellent captive environment for these robust lizards (Figure 12 a–c). Such an arrangement can, of course, be scaled down accordingly.

Figure 12 a & b—see page 86.

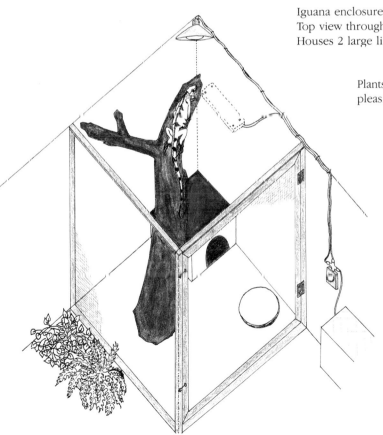

Iguana enclosure built against a corner of a room.
Top view through the ceiling; 1″ = about 1½′.
Houses 2 large lizards comfortably.

Plants provide extra humidity and are aesthetically pleasing to people and lizards.

Heat lamp, vitalite and a humidifier are plugged into an automatic timer *outside* the cage.

Wires are affixed to ceiling and wall

Figure 12 c. A non-institutional environmental suitable for a pet iguana. Illustration by W. Townsend.

WASTE MANAGEMENT

Maintenance supplies required for collections of multiple iguanas should include a plastic tub of cleaning supplies, a stack of newspapers, and a trash can which is kept outside the iguana room. In the tub are: a roll of paper towels, a plastic scrub brush, a container of bleach, and a little plastic bowl for the water and bleach solution which is prepared as needed. Kitchen sponges that are no longer fresh may be recycled through use in the iguana room.

Droppings that miss the newspapers are picked up with paper towel and disposed of in the toilet; the residue is easily removed with the bleach solution and sponge. Iguanas are clean animals and have no distinct body odor. They lift their tails clear during defecation, but may later scatter feces, food, or anything else in their path of activity. A vacuum cleaner is invaluable for periodic cleanings and doesn't bother the iguanas. While iguanas cannot be disciplined to toilet like a cat or dog, they will generally use a particular place repeatedly. A water bowl, tray of sand or kitty litter, or newspapers can be placed strategically to facilitate cleaning chores. Although coarse sand or cat litter is often used as a depository for wastes, these substances are *not* suitable for a cage substrate because they are easily ingested along with food and can cause gastrointestinal obstructions. Also, remember, if newspaper is used to cover a toileting area, important documents must not be left unattended where they can be similarly soiled; few iguanas have learned to read! Some iguanas prefer to employ their water bowl or your bathtub for this purpose. All wastes and the water from the iguana's water bowl should be disposed of in the toilet, not the kitchen sink. Feces, urinary wastes, uneaten food, remnants of shed skin, etc. provide a fertile medium in which disease-causing bacteria and fungi can thrive, and fecal wastes from worm-infected iguanas can serve to transmit parasites from one lizard to another.

Professional and sophisticated amateur herpetologists follow a routine cage cleaning and renovation program on a regular basis. This program also provides an opportunity to record feeding and elimination by individual animals so that any abnormalities in intake or output become immediately apparent. One or two bowel movements daily, depending upon the lizard's growth, can be considered normal and healthy elimination for iguanas.

All utensils that are employed for cleaning cages should be thoroughly cleansed after each use before being used in another cage. A solution of common household bleach (sodium hypochlorite) is recommended for this purpose because it is highly effective against a wide variety of disease-causing organisms. Generally, use the manufacturer's recommended dilutions for sanitation purposes. Similarly, all nondisposable plates used for feeding must be sanitized and rinsed well with fresh water before being returned to the cage.

Among other items that should be kept on hand are povidone iodine solution (Betadine® or its equivalent generic form), 3% hydrogen peroxide, and Neosporin® creme (rather than ointment). The liquid bandage NewSkin® is useful for treating abrasions and lacerations.

It may seem that good iguana husbandry requires a great deal of time and effort. Depending upon the number of lizards one keeps, the basic maintenance routine is established and soon becomes second nature, requiring a modest amount of time. While a lot of time is spent "playing" with a group of iguanas, taking them out for sunshine, letting them swim in the bathtub, and also just sitting and watching them, one should expect to spend about one hour every other day on basic care.

If an outdoor enclosure is used to house iguanas, it is generally a good husbandry practice to move the site where food is offered daily so that there is no accumulation of uneaten food. Exposing these sites to unfiltered sunlight has a sanitizing effect.

ENVIRONMENTAL TEMPERATURE

All reptiles possess a critical high temperature beyond which they will perish. Iguanas thermoregulate by behavior and can only warm up or cool down by moving close to or away from a given heat source. Maintaining a lizard at or near its critical high temperature is stressful and should be avoided. Any enclosure for iguanas should afford a temperature gradient, giving the lizards options. Although iguanas will move to shade or water to cool down, no object or surface that an iguana may come into contact with should exceed 38° C (100° F) because the lizard may be unwittingly burned. Generally, the tropical rain forest and tropical island dwelling species of iguanas should be kept so that their warmest daytime temperature during the summer months is maintained at from approximately 27° C–34° C (80°–94° F). Some variance during the 12–14 hour day is desirable; the mornings and later afternoons should be cooler than the midday temperatures; this variance will encourage the lizards to alter their activity patterns to include basking.

With outdoor enclosures, maintaining these temperatures is relatively simple if sufficient shade is provided. Iguanas housed in outdoor habitats exposed to natural sunlight and frequent natural or artificial rain showers are more likely to feed better and reproduce more readily. Lizards kept indoors will require more elaborate housing utilizing subsurface heaters, full-spectrum ultraviolet illumination and artificial incandescent lights to furnish "hot-spots" in which to bask and thermoregulate adequately to meet their temperature requirements. Several of these basking spots should be provided if more than one lizard is occupying the cage in order to help prevent disputes over favored territory where lizards can seek warmth or social dominance. More information will be presented later about the provision of sufficient "hot-spots" for each iguana in a group.

HUMIDITY

Because the native habitats of many of the tropical iguanine lizards are rain forests, the need for maintaining adequate humidity is important. Generally, a relative humidity for these tropical iguanas should be 85–95%. The desert-dwelling *Dipsosaurus dorsalis* and the chuckawallas of the genus *Sauromalus* should be maintained at a relative humidity of 35–50% maximum. The spiny-tailed iguanas, *Ctenosaurus* sp., live in a habitat that may be relatively humid at night and in the early morning hours, but tends to become much dryer during the warmest portion of the day; for these lizards, a relative humidity of 60–85% appears to be ideal.

Outdoor enclosures may be sprayed daily or twice daily to simulate natural rain showers. Large indoor cages can have their humidity controlled by including an air humidifier, or in smaller cages, the air can be humidified by placing a shallow container of water over a heating source such as a subcage heating pad. Adding living plants to an indoor terrarium will also increase the relative humidity of the cage air and provide security for juvenile lizards. However, small potted plants will be promptly trampled and LOVED to death by a large iguana. Three or four leafy hanging plants such as wandering Jew (*Zebrina pendula*), or pothos (*Epipremnum aureum*) are excellent for humidifying an area where large iguanas are living. As noted earlier, pothos are noxious, but iguanas soon learn to leave them alone. Only safe plants should be used for this purpose; consult Table 3 for a list of toxic plants to be avoided.

CAGE LITTER MATERIALS

Under natural conditions, tropical iguanas walk on the forest floor, and move about on a surface consisting of fallen leaves in various stages of decomposition, rotting branches and logs, a myriad of fungi, and composted soil. Ground and rock iguanas are native to islands with varying amounts of relatively organic compost-poor sandy soil and large boulder-size rocks. Desert iguanas and chuckawallas live in more sandy and rocky habitats, often with sparse vegetation. Outdoor habitats should attempt to mimic these broadly outlined parameters. Indoor enclosures pose more difficulties, but can be furnished so that they meet the requirements for the animals, are practical to construct and maintain, and are aesthetically pleasing. However, one must be careful to avoid creating a "natural" habitat that also is a hazard to its inhabitants. For instance, fine sand and small pebbles are easily swallowed along with food items and can result in gastrointestinal upset, obstruction, and eventual death of the animals who ingest them. The terms *geophagy* (earth or soil eating) and *lithophagy* (stone eating) refer to the habit of some iguanas to ingest foreign materials they find in their cages or enclosures. Figure 13 illustrates an x-ray photograph of a mature chuckawalla whose stomach and intestines contain numerous rocks and stones that it had ingested. As lizards move along the ground tongue-testing various surfaces, they sometimes nibble on or eat dust, sand, or soil. This behavior may signal a mineral deficiency; therefore, an animal who repeatedly ingests these materials should be evaluated by a veterinarian because they can create gastrointestinal obstructions. Similarly, ground corn cob litter, clay kitty litter, wood shavings, etc. can, if swallowed, cause blockages. Note that while cat litter or sand are suitable for use in a litter tray or pan in the iguana's toilet area, these are NOT recommended as a cage substrate. Instead, use clean newspaper, butcher's wrap, paper toweling, artificial turf-type indoor-outdoor carpeting or, best of all, although it is not aesthetically attractive, use pelleted ground alfalfa, which is not only digestible, but also nutritious. It must be changed whenever it becomes moistened or soiled with fecal matter.

Figure 13—see page 86.

FURNISHING THE CAGE

Trees, large branches, or artificial trees should be provided so that the iguanas will have ample places to rest, bask, and display social interactions among themselves. Tree trunks, branches, etc. should either be living or well secured so that they will not topple over and crush the inhabitants. The type of tree or branch is vitally important; resinous trees such as pine, fir, cedar, redwood, eucalyptus, etc. should be avoided. Most hard fruit woods are ideal, as are rough-barked oaks because they offer a good gripping surface for the lizards' sharp claws. Avoid smooth-surfaced tree varieties such as manzanita and madrone because, although they are nonresinous, their bark is so smooth and slick that lizards may lose their grip and fall, often breaking their bones. If there is sufficient room, a sturdy living plant such as a hibiscus or mulberry tree is ideal. Any branch that has been lying on the ground should be discarded; also avoid decaying or brittle branches which might break under the weight of a large iguana. Sturdy dead tree trunks or branches should be sanitized with household bleach, rinsed thoroughly with water, and dried completely before being installed in the cage.

It is often the manner in which food is presented that enhances the likelihood of accidental litter ingestion. Placing soft wet food items such as fresh fruit and vegetables directly on sand or pebbles may result in these litter materials being taken in with the food. It would be better to place the food in a shallow platter or bowl so that it can be eaten without having adherent particulate materials. In outdoor enclosures, food can be presented on a bed of fresh grass or clean edible leaves.

FURTHER CONSIDERATIONS

Having learned some of the "dos" and "don'ts" via a variety of housing trials and errors, the junior author wishes to make a few more recommendations with respect to the general care and maintenance of the green iguana.

Townsend's Corollaries to Murphy's law of reptile keeping:

If an escape is even remotely possible, it will happen.

If there is any way that a reptile can harm itself, it usually will.

Think prevention and observe your animal(s) regularly.

One need not become overly concerned about this, but be aware of ANY potential hazard to the pet. For example, if planning an outdoor enclosure, ask yourself: Could a free-roaming dog or coyote gain access to the yard? Smaller iguanas periodically fall prey to pet or feral cats and, depending on your location, the possibility of a lizard being carried off by a raptor such as a hawk or owl is not out of the question. If these mishaps are even remotely likely to happen, you should construct a particularly sturdy enclosure with some provision for screening out cats, foxes, weasels, skunks, raccoons, hawks and owls. At any rate, only large iguanas with at least 36 cm (14-inches) snout-vent length (SVL) should be allowed to roam an open outdoor area.

When setting up an indoor room, determine if the iguana could climb any furniture or drapery to get to an open or poorly screened window and escape. If so, rearrange the room, keeping in mind that iguanas can leap a fair distance.

Iguanas smaller than about 30 cm (12-inches) SVL should be kept within an enclosure for their protection. A small iguana could stray into areas where he may not be found, may be stepped on, injured by the movement of furniture, or attacked by other household pets. Young iguanas grow rapidly during the first years of life and, if properly raised, reach 30 cm SVL by the first year. You can avoid having to purchase and set up progressively larger tanks to accommodate a lizard's increasing size by initially investing in a glass or plexiglass tank of no less than a 220 liter (55 gallon) capacity. Another option is to construct a cage of similar volume.

While iguanas don't require a lot of open space to be "happy," they don't especially like enclosures. However well-adjusted a pet iguana becomes to its confines, it will spend a fair portion of time pacing and digging at the boundaries as long as it can see that it's in an enclosure (its tank or cage) within an enclosure (the room). It is recommended that a "cageless" setup be planned for your iguana when it is between 2 and 3 years old. Once out of a cage, the tame iguana will cease pacing, and will usually remain within an area that is to its liking. Such an area includes heat, security and food.

When constructing an enclosure, hardware cloth with half-inch mesh is recommended for all parts of a cage that are to be screened, such as a lid or door. Chicken wire will not contain a small baby iguana and regular window screening is too fine because the iguana will inevitably catch one or more of its claws in its woven mesh. Once a young iguana that had been kept in a bedroom was found hanging from a finely screened cage lid by a single toe. As he was dangling there, his posture appeared humorous—as if he'd been caught in the middle of something. He had been scratching at the lid, gotten stuck and, in his struggles to get free, twisted and broke his toe, which turned black after a few days and had to be amputated.

Chicken wire has been employed to partition off an area of a room for large iguanas. This was a successful arrangement because the lizards apparently did not perceive that they were caged. The partition was there only to prevent them from exploring a roommate's property!

A lesson was learned about "cutting corners" when preparing an iguana home. A few years ago, three of the junior author's iguanas each lost a toenail or two by wedging them between two pieces of metal that formed the door to a cage. This cage was thought to be a grand design. It was inexpensive, easy to assemble, clean and, best of all, it closely resembled the previous cage that had worked out so well, but had been too large and heavy to move. This new cage was actually an elevated rabbit hutch that was adjusted to meet the iguanas' needs. Two small iguanas were housed within, protected from four other large lizards that would climb up and bask on top of the cage. For nearly a month all was well until the day I went into the room and found blood all over the newspapers and one of the iguanas who was flexing a forelimb with only four toenails on it. Two days and three more toenails later, the little place which caused the damage was found. It was amazing that the cage lasted as long as it did because it was a mistake to have kept the cage as long as I had; I found several places where such injuries could occur. Out went the nifty new hutch, and I had to start from scratch.

Another apartment without a partition or similar structure was once used to contain iguanas. They spent most of the time basking on top of a cage the size and shape of a large refrigerator. Now and then one of the lizards would come down to drink, eat, or explore the room, and would then return to the top of the cage.

Over the years of sharing various rooms with two or more large iguanas, one learns to expect the unexpected. For example, though iguanas will spend most of the time basking or remaining within their "area," there will inevitably be a time or two when a lizard will discover either the long silk dress hanging temptingly in the closet, or the collection of little fragile items on an accessible shelf. More than a few times an owner has come home to find an iguana happily clinging—with sharp claws—to the delicate fabric of a once-favored garment (here again would be the same humorous posture of the lizard caught in the middle of something . . .), or to the remains of a much-treasured glass frog collection.

If you plan to share your room with one or more large iguanas, keep fragile or valued objects out of reach, or build a partition.

When a pet iguana strays from its area, it may be looking for a secure place to hide. If there is no suitable sleeping place within the iguana's area, it may pace and dig at its boundaries, especially if it can see a corner or shelf it would like to get to. Toward the end of daylight, even in an artificially illuminated environment, iguanas begin to seek out what they perceive to be a safe place to sleep. In the wild, this would likely be a branch high off the ground draped by the foliage of other branches. Before settling upon the right hiding places, your iguanas might seek out particular cabinets, closets or shelves in or on which to sleep. Iguanas have good spatial recollection and sense of direction. In an apartment or home, they remember having seen spaces behind closed doors or such, and will persist at getting into a desired location. Bird houses or cardboard boxes make nice hiding places for small lizards. Dog houses come in different sizes and make excellent hiding places for larger iguanas.

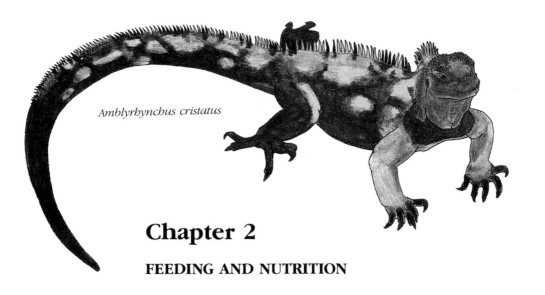

Amblyrhynchus cristatus

Chapter 2

FEEDING AND NUTRITION

Water Requirements, Dehydration, and Gout

The necessity to drink water depends largely upon the moisture content in the dietary items, "insensitive" water loss to the environment through the respiratory system, and the nature of an animal's urinary and fecal wastes. For example, lizards fed diets containing soft fruits, melons, and other foods containing a low percentage of dry matter excrete soft, moisture-laden stools. When fed a diet rich in high dry-matter food items such as leaves, they excrete much drier feces and chalky urinary wastes from which much moisture has been extracted. Many desert-dwelling reptiles are capable of recycling considerable amounts of water from the urinary wastes while they are stored in the urinary bladder. These characteristics, together with the complementary action of salt excreting glands (discussed later) in conserving water, make it possible for many reptiles to survive in some extremely harsh and arid habitats.

Much of a reptile's body water economy is derived from the moisture contained in its food, but most species will drink an additional volume of water IF it is presented in an acceptable form and manner. Many reptiles will refuse to drink voluntarily from containers of standing water. In nature, most iguanas—with the exception of the marine iguana—drink moisture as rain or dewdroplets. Some will drink water only by lapping dew-like drops from misted foliage; some can be trained to imbibe fresh water from shallow vessels. Both hatchling and newly acquired iguanas should be "shown" their water bowl daily during the first few weeks of captivity. Splash the surface of the water with a finger while the iguana is nearby, and it will likely take a drink.

Frequently, captive lizards will soak for prolonged periods in their water containers but, contrary to popular opinion, they do *not* absorb water in a sponge-like fashion during this activity. Soaking promotes bowel activity, and is also apparently pleasurable to iguanas. A sturdy water bowl that won't be easily tipped and that can accommodate at least half the lizard's body should be made available. Iguanas will usually defecate in water, which can facilitate cleaning chores. Change dirtied water promptly, remembering to clean and rinse the bowl thoroughly. Whether dirty or not, refresh water at least daily.

Some reptiles possess highly specialized extra-renal sodium, potassium and chloride-secreting "salt glands." These glandular structures produce a concentrated or *hypertonic* secretion, thus aiding in the conservation of precious water stores by removing excess salts without the loss of significant amounts of water. Dried salt crystals are sometimes observed around the nostrils (Figure 14 a & b).

Figure 14 a—see page 87.

A relative or absolute deficiency of *metabolically available* water often leads to dehydration and the accumulation of insoluble sodium, potassium, and ammonium urate salts within the kidneys and other tissue sites. When gently pinched, the skin of a dehydrated iguana will remain elevated for a few moments. Replacement fluid should be administered at a volume of 15–25 ml/kg every 24 hours.

In the case of terrestrial lizards, the concentrations of urates may promote the formation of urinary bladder stones which occasionally reach enormous size.

Figure 14 b. Dried droplets of salt-laden secretion can be seen on the inner surfaces of this terrarium. Photo by W. Townsend.

Because of the intimate relationship between water and the excretion of nitrogenous urinary waste products, it is important to understand the fate of nitrogen-rich food sources after they are eaten. In most reptiles, the end products of such nitrogenous foods are salts of uric acid. These urate salts are the biochemical residues resulting from the reaction of uric acid with sodium, potassium, and ammonium ions in the body fluids. In carnivorous reptiles, the plasma uric acid rises dramatically a day or two after eating a protein-rich meal and then quickly returns to a prefeeding level. In herbivorous and omnivorous reptiles, particularly those whose proteinaceous nitrogen is derived from plant sources, uric acid reaches the peak level and returns to the prefeeding state over a longer time. Therefore, an iguana who is already moderately dehydrated is placed at a greater risk of uric acid accumulation than one which is properly hydrated.

As long as the blood circulation to the kidneys is adequate to maintain the clearance of urate salts, accumulation is unlikely to occur; however, because of the insolubility of these salts, many reptiles are placed at substantial risk of inflammation of joints and/or internal organs due to gout after experiencing water deprivation. Thus, *it is absolutely essential that fresh water is always readily available to all captive iguanas.*

FEEDING AND NUTRITION

For captive iguanas, good health and development are especially dependent upon a balanced diet. Many illnesses and even injuries result from nutritional deficiencies. Early signs of malnutrition include slow, if any, growth, lackluster skin, brittle bones, thinness, lack of appetite, and overall apathetic behavior. It can take either a few months or even a year for an iguana to die of severe malnutrition. Iguanas with milder deficiencies can live for several years, but usually suffer from ailments that often go unnoticed. Proper nutrition is preventive and easy to provide, once understood.

Seven of the eight genera of iguanid lizards tend to prefer vegetation in one form or another as well as varying amounts of animal tissues; the lone exception is the marine iguana, *Amblyrhynchus cristatus*. As noted in the Introduction, iguanas can discern the colors red, yellow, orange, and green; therefore, this information is used to prepare diets that are visually attractive to these lizards.

Iguanas may, depending upon their natural habits and species, confine their diet to vegetable matter (leaves, blossoms, fruits), or animal protein (in the form of other lizards, small birds, mammals, carrion, molluscs, gastropods, insects and arachnids, or eggs), or a combination of several basic food classes. Some iguanas change their dietary preferences as they mature. For example, when young the common green iguana, *Iguana iguana*, hunts eagerly for insects and arachnids, but will also consume leaves, blossoms, and fruit. As an adult, it prefers fruits and leafy vegetables, but will accept small mammals and eggs if they are offered. Some iguanas are highly specialized in their dietary preferences. For instance, the marine iguana, *Amblyrhynchus cristatus*, eats a diet consisting largely of seaweed, tender kelp, and marine grasses and algae; occasional fish and molluscs also may be eaten. This lizard dives for its meals, grazing upon the rocky shore and associated sandy bottom. It is able to swim without surfacing for approximately 30 minutes, all the while plucking tender marine vegetation; its blunt head enables it to crop this plant growth closely from rocky surfaces. Other iguanas tend to be more omnivorous in their food preferences. Most are well developed to process cellulose-rich leafy plant material, tender blossoms, soft fruits, and cactus.

Many of these lizards will also eagerly seek out and consume food of animal origin. Insects, arachnids, snails, small mammals, bird eggs and nestlings and, occasionally, other lizards are eaten. Several of the ground iguanas eat carrion, including dead mammals, fish, and crustaceans; the senior author has twice found old rusted fishhooks in wild, caught rock and ground iguanas from the Caribbean. For the readers' convenience, we have included graphs of food preferences (Figure 15).

Small items are swallowed whole; larger pieces are torn into bitesized portions. Some lizards chew their food before swallowing it. If two or more iguanas are housed together, it is better to place the food in more than one plate, bowl, or pile because this will help avoid disputes over favored food items.

Another option is to prepare a thoroughly combined mixture or salad of foods, which eliminates vitamin supplement waste and ensures that each "bite" is complete. This, too, is advantageous and convenient if two or more iguanas, or a large group of lizards varying in size, are being fed. After several meals, the amount of food that needs to be prepared becomes clear.

Because they are true folivores (leaf-eaters), the common green iguanas thrive on a diet of moistened pelleted alfalfa rabbit or guinea pig chow, dandelion blossoms and leaves, rose petals, tender chopped turnip, collard or mustard greens, and tender fig, eugenia, hibiscus and mulberry (*Morus*) leaves, thawed frozen mixed vegetables, fresh fruit (sliced apples, pears, pitted stone fruits, ripe papaya, grated squash, melons, etc.), tofu soybean cake, occasional crickets, silk moth larvae, baby mouse pups, chopped hard-cooked eggs, and small amounts of commercial dog or cat food—not exceeding 5% of the total ration; but the bulk of the diet should come from leafy vegetables and fruit. Commercially prepared pet foods, which are designed to meet the nutritional requirements of carnivores, contain substantial amounts of vitamins A and D that greatly exceed the requirements (and tolerance) of herbivorous lizards. When fed to excess, dog or cat food may induce lesions of arteriosclerosis in reptiles.

If available in sufficient quantities, some commonly grown houseplants, especially hibiscus, nasturtium, and the ubiquitous wandering Jew, *Zebrina pendula*, are avidly eaten and are highly nutritious for these leaf-eating lizards. As noted earlier, adult common green, Fiji, rock, and ground iguanas tend to prefer a more herbivorous diet than juveniles of these species, which are far more carnivorous. Usually by the end of their first year in their native habitat, juvenile iguanas begin their gradual dietary preference change to tender shoots, blossoms, and other plant parts, rounding out their intake with ever-lessening amounts of animal protein. (See Auffenberg, 1982; Hirth, 1963; Iverson, 1982; Loftin and Tyson, 1965;

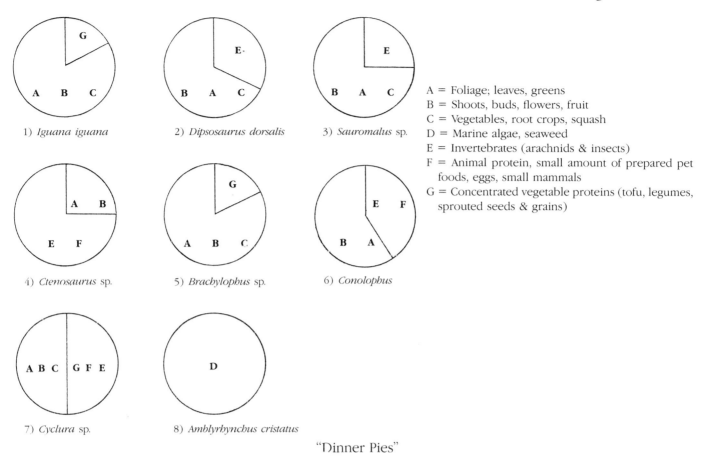

A = Foliage; leaves, greens
B = Shoots, buds, flowers, fruit
C = Vegetables, root crops, squash
D = Marine algae, seaweed
E = Invertebrates (arachnids & insects)
F = Animal protein, small amount of prepared pet foods, eggs, small mammals
G = Concentrated vegetable proteins (tofu, legumes, sprouted seeds & grains)

1) *Iguana iguana* 2) *Dipsosaurus dorsalis* 3) *Sauromalus* sp.

4) *Ctenosaurus* sp. 5) *Brachylophus* sp. 6) *Conolophus*

7) *Cyclura* sp. 8) *Amblyrhynchus cristatus*

"Dinner Pies"

Figure 15. Approximate proportions of vegetable material and protein sources that captive iguanine lizards should be fed. The larger proportion of each lettered category is listed from left to right.

McBee and McBee, 1982; Montgomery, 1978; Rand, 1978; Rand, et al., 1990; Sylber, 1988; Troyer, 1982, 1984; and VanDevender, 1982.)

Hatchling common iguanas have been observed in the wild actively ingesting fresh feces from older conspecific lizards. Troyer (1982) reported that this behavior was directly related to the acquisition of symbiotic microbes necessary for the fermentative processing of cellulose and other carbohydrates. In those iguanas that prefer to eat leafy vegetables and soft fruits, a balanced vitamin-mineral supplement that is rich in calcium carbonate usually is administered once or twice weekly by mixing an appropriate amount with the soft food or fruit puree. Even the leaf-eating iguanas usually will accept insects such as silk-moth larvae which contain substantial amounts of valuable calcium in their tissues.

Iguanas with less specialized diets may benefit from a varied diet. Factors influencing these differences in nutritional quality are water content, energy content per dry weight, and assimilation energy efficiencies.

For instance, iceberg lettuce is an example of a high-water content, low-nutritional quality item. Moreover, the relative amounts of calcium and phosphorus of head lettuce are reversed and, if iceberg lettuce is fed to excess, metabolic disturbances are likely to occur. Food items that are high in easily digested and assimilated carbohydrate tend to foster obesity, fermentation, and excessive intestinal gas production.

Green, desert, Fiji, spiny-tailed, rock, and ground iguanas, as well as chuckawallas, thrive on a diet of chopped mixed green leafy vegetables such as collard, kale, turnip, mustard, dandelion leaves and flowers, broccoli leaves, mixed soft stone fruits, apples, pears, papaya, mango, melons, etc. Freshly thawed mixed vegetables, tender mulberry leaves, hibiscus leaves and flowers, small pieces of slightly softened stale whole multigrain bread, and mixed bean, pea, lentil, and pulse sprouts round out the menu. Many of these food items can be obtained free as slightly wilted vegetables from your grocer; others can be grown or collected in your neighborhood. The bean, pea, lentil and pulse sprouts are easily produced in your kitchen (Frye, 1991b); this information is reprinted later in this text. Figure 16 illustrates a variety of attractive and nutritious food items that are ideal for many iguanine species.

Figure 16—see page 87.

Generally, iguanas are fed free choice several times weekly. Younger lizards, because they are growing rapidly, need to feed more often; older, mature lizards can be maintained on a three to four times per week feeding schedule. Specifically, hatchlings measuring from approximately 8.5 cm (3.3 inches) SVL should be fed daily; yearlings measuring approximately 17.5 cm (7 inches) SVL should eat at least five times weekly; and adult green iguanas three-years-old and older who measure approximately 35 cm (14 inches) SVL usually should be fed three or four times weekly. Also, the frequency of feeding depends upon the activity level of the lizards, their reproductive status, and the nutritive density or quality of the diet. The effect of the reproductive status on the appetite and nutritional requirements of mature iguanas is discussed in the **REPRODUCTION** section of this text. The *quality* of the foodstuffs also plays a major role in determining the amount of any ration fed to these animals. For instance, a diet consisting of high-water content foods like melons, and some fresh fruits contains less cellulose and other nutrients than a diet whose identical weight consists of fresh leaves or grain-rich bread.

To give an example of a dietary routine, the junior author includes the following recipe, as well as a few practical suggestions for food selection, preparation and storage:

Every two or three days, I prepare the following salad for my iguanas. I put aside about a cup of the mixture in a plastic storage container in the refrigerator to feed to the two smaller iguanas for their daily meals. The rest of the salad is usually consumed by the adults in one feeding. If you have only one iguana, use small amounts of each item and store the preparation in the refrigerator. Make a fresh batch after three days. Alternatively, you can feed individual food items a few at a time, taking care to provide variety as well as sufficient nutrition.

A meal preparation for 8 green iguanas: 2 small, 2 medium and 4 large. While fixing produce, soak with ½ cup water in a large bowl:

⅓ cup alfalfa pellets

1 slice whole grain bread (I like to use the "flourless" varieties, available in health food stores and some super markets).

Add:

3 cups shredded dark greens, one to three varieties, such as: dandelion, beet, collard, mustard or kale*

⅔ cup grated vegetable, one or two varieties, such as: pumpkin, carrot, sweet potato, yellow squash, or broccoli

1 cup grated or mashed fruit, one variety, such as: cactus pear, apple, fresh fig, pear, plum, papaya

Every second or third preparation, add:

⅔ cup tofu or sprouted sunflower seeds, buckwheat or mung beans

3–4 tablespoons monkey chow or dog food (I like to use Science Diet . . . [see discussion on the overfeeding of commercially prepared foods formulated for mammals])

1 teaspoon calcium carbonate powder

1 teaspoon Zoovite®, Reptivite®, Supergreen®, Vionate® or other multivitamin/mineral. Store vitamin-mineral supplements under refrigeration to ensure their freshness and potency.

Combine all and serve. I prefer to use my hands for the mixing as it's thorough and warms the food in the process. Food should be room temperature before it is presented to iguanas. A salad recipe follows within this chapter.

Iguanas will acquire a taste for almost any food offered constantly regardless of its nutritional value, or even detrimental qualities. Care must be taken not to begin feeding captive lizards the wrong foods. Refer to Table 2, Table 3, and the list of nutritious plant materials and sample diets in this chapter for guidelines in planning a good dietary routine. If an iguana is already eating poor or deficient foods, a transition to a healthier diet should be made by mixing a little of the usual poor food with the new good

---

*Either mince or remove thick stems of greens because, if left whole, these can cause an iguana's gums to bleed as they masticate. Overfeeding kale and other cabbage-like plants can induce thyroid disorders.

EXAMPLES OF PLANT MATERIALS THAT ARE SAFE AND NUTRITIOUS

Alfalfa: fresh, sun-cured hay, dried leaves, pellets, meal

Apple: fresh, with peel, sliced or grated (discard core and seeds)

Barley: freshly sprouted seeds, freshly grown leaves, sun-cured hay

Beans (several edible varieties): fresh leaves and stems, fruit

Bean sprouts (adzuki, black-eyed, garbanzo, lentil, mung, pea, etc.): fresh leaves, stems, blossoms, fruit

Beet: tops, stems, flowers, grated roots

Berseem (Egyptian clover): leaves, sun-cured hay

Blackberry: tender leaves, berries

Buffalo grass (*Bulbilis dactyloides*): hay

Cabbage family (kale, napa, broccoli, Brussel's sprouts): do not feed to excess.

Cactus: flowers, prickly pears, tender young cactus pads

Carrot: leaves, grated root

Clover (Ladino, Alsike, etc.): fresh, sun-cured hay

Collards: fresh green leaves, flowers

Cotton: leaves, dried or fresh

Cowpea: sun-cured hay, leaves

Crucifers (Brassicaceae): bok choy, etc.

Dandelion: leaves and stems, flowers, fresh or dried

Dicondra: fresh or sun-cured hay

Eugenia: fresh leaves, fruits

Figs: fresh

Grass clippings: freshly mowed or sun-cured

Hibiscus: leaves, flowers, fresh pods

Kudzu: sun-cured hay

Lespedeza: sun-cured hay, leaves

Millet: leaves, sun-cured hay

Mint: sun-cured hay

Mixed vegetables: frozen, thawed

Mulberry: freshly picked tender leaves, fruit

Mustard: fresh green leaves, flowers

Nasturtium: leaves, stems, flowers

Okra: fresh, chopped, tender leaves and blossoms

Pea: fresh pods, sun-cured hay

Pear: fresh, cut or grated (discard core and seeds)

Peavine: sun-cured hay

Peanut: sun-cured hay with or without nuts

Pelleted commercial chows (Purina, Wayne, etc.) for guinea pigs and rabbits can be fed *ad lib*; those formulated for horses, goats, dogs, cats or monkeys, etc. *SHOULD NOT BE FED IN EXCESS*

Rape: fresh leaves, sun-cured hay

Rutabaga: freshly grated root

Saltbush (winter range): sun-cured hay

Soybean: fresh leaves or sun-cured hay

Squash: freshly grated flesh, blossoms, tender leaves

Stone fruits: peach, nectarine, apricot, plum, etc. (discard seeds)

Sunflower: seeds (unsalted)

Timothy: sun-cured hay

Tofu soybean cake

Triticale: freshly sprouted seeds, sun-cured hay

Turnip: fresh leaves, grated root

Vetch: sun-cured hay

Wheat (soft wheat berries): freshly sprouted, hydroponically grown

From Frye, (1991b)

TABLE 2
Food Preferences for Iguanas

Iguana species	SM	B	I	E	CM	M/G	FISH	F	V
Chuckawalla	O		O	O	O			X	X
Sauromalus obesus; S. ater;				boiled					
S. varius; S. hispidus									
Common green*	O	O	X	X	O	O		X	X
Iguana iguana; I. i. rhinolopha						snails			esp. leafy
Desert	O	X			O	O		X	X
Dipsosaurus dorsalis									
Fiji	O	O	X	O	O	O		X	X
Brachylophus fasciatus;									
B. vitiensis									
Ground, Rhinoceros	X	O	X	O	O	O	X	X	X
Cyclura sp., (several)									
Conolophus pallidus;									
C. subcristatus									
Marine						O	X		algae
Amblyrhynchus cristatus									& kelp
Spiny-tailed	X		O			O		X	X
Ctenosaura pectinata;						snails			leaves, blossoms,
C. sp.									& fruit

*diet varies see text
Legend: X = usual food items; O = occasionally eaten; SM = small mammals; B = birds (chicks); I = insects & arachnids; E = eggs; CM = chopped meat(s); M/G = mollusks/gastropods; FISH = miscellaneous fish including fish carrion; F = fruit; V = vegetables
modified from Frye, (1991 b).

food so that the iguana will eat his meal. Gradually reduce the amount of the former diet until it is totally replaced by the proper foods. A discussion on correcting bad dietary habits with seed sprouts is given later in this chapter.

Iguanas should be fed between 11:00 a.m. and 2:00 p.m., as they feed most heartily after warming up and then have the afternoon to bask and digest. The bacteria and protozoa responsible for digestion of plant matter prior to nutrient absorption operate optimally in the mid- to upper 90s° F. If you must feed your iguana late in the day, make sure a hot spot is available so he can do his basking for an hour or two after the meal.

Sometimes, organically grown produce is fed, but this is not critical or always convenient. Generally, health food stores, organic grocers and farmer's markets have high quality fruits and vegetables. Always be on the lookout for local forage (nontoxic!), such as wild blackberries and hibiscus and dandelion flowers, as well as special fruits or flowers that become available at the supermarket, such as blueberries or squash blossoms.

As a guideline, deep colors are usually indicative of superior nutrient and flavor content in produce. Avoid "using up" fading, yellowed greens

TABLE 3
Food values

Food	Measure	A units	B-1 (mg)	B-2 (mg)	C (mg)	Calc. (mg)	Phos. (mg)	Iron (mg)	Prot. (gm)
			Vitamins			Minerals			Other
apple	1 small	90	.360	.050	6	7	12	0.3	0
apricot #	3 med.	7,500	.033	.100	4	13	24	0.6	1
asparagus	8 stks	1,100	.360	.065	20	21	40	1.0	2
avocado	1/2 med	500	.120	.137	9	44	42	6.3	2
banana	1 med.	300	.045	.087	10	8	28	0.6	1
beans, grn*	3/4 cup	950	.060	.100	8	55	50	1.1	2
beet greens*	1/2 cup	22,000	.100	.500	50	94	40	3.2	2
beets	1/2 cup	50	.041	.037	8	28	42	2.8	2
blackberries	3/4 cup	300	.025	.030	3	32	32	0.9	0
blueberries	3/4 cup	35	.045	.031	11	25	20	0.9	0
broccoli flr	3/4 cup	6,500	.120	.350	65	64	105	1.3	2
broccoli leaf	3/4 cup	30,000	.120	.687	90	262	67	2.3	3
broccoli stem	3/4 cup	2,000	—	.187	—	83	35	1.1	2
brussels spr	3/4 cup	400	.180	.090	130	27	121	2.1	4
cabbage (1)	1 cup	0	.780	.075	50	46	34	2.0	2
cabbage (2)	1 cup	160	.090	.150	50	429	72	2.8	2
cabbage (3)	1 cup	5,000	.036	.462	50	400	72	2.5	2
cataloupe	1/2 small	900	.090	.100	50	32	30	0.5	1
carrots (4)	1/2 cup	4,500	.070	.075	5	45	41	0.6	1
cauliflower	3/4 cup	10	.085	.090	75	122	60	0.9	2
celery (5)	4 stlk	20	.030	.015	5	78	46	0.5	1
celery, grn	4 stlk	640	.030	.045	7	98	46	0.8	1
celery root	1/2 cup	—	—	—	2	47	71	0.8	3
chard, lvs*	1/2 cup	15,000	.450	.165	37	150	50	3.1	2
cherries #	12 lrg	259	.051	—	12	19	30	0.4	1
collards *	1/2 cup	6,300	.130	—	70	207	75	3.4	3
corn on cob	1 med.	860	.209	.055	8	8	103	0.4	3
cucumber	1 med.	35	.060	.054	12	10	21	0.3	1
dandelion grn*	1/2 cup	20,000	.190	.270	100	84	35	0.6	3
eggplant	1/2 cup	70	.042	.036	10	11	31	0.5	1
endive	10 stks	15,000	.058	.072	20	104	39	1.2	1
grapefruit	1/2 med.	20	.070	.060	45	21	20	0.2	0
grapes	1 sm bnch	25	.030	.024	3	19	35	0.7	1
guavas	1	200	.156	.105	125	15	16	3.0	1
honeydew melon	1/4 med.	100	—	—	90	—	—	—	0
huckleberry	1/2 cup	100	.045	.021	8	25	20	0.2	1
kale*	1/2 cup	20,000	.189	.570	96	195	67	2.5	4
kohlrabi	1/2 cup	—	.030	.120	50	195	60	0.7	2
leeks	1/2 cup	20	.150	—	24	58	56	0.6	2
lettuce, grn	10 lvs	2,000	.075	.150	7	49	28	1.5	1
lettuce, wht	1/4 head	125	.051	.062	5	17	40	0.5	1
mushrooms (6)	3/4 cup	0	.160	.070	2	14	98	0.7	4
mustard gr.	1/2 cup	11,000	.138	.450	126	291	84	9.1	2
okra	1/2 cup	440	.126	—	17	72	62	2.1	2
onions, frsh	4 med.	60	.042	.125	7	41	47	0.4	1
orange	1 med.	190	.090	.075	50	44	18	0.4	0

TABLE 3
Food values (continued)

Food	Measure	A units	Vitamins			Minerals			Other
			B-1 (mg)	B-2 (mg)	C (mg)	Calc. (mg)	Phos. (mg)	Iron (mg)	Prot. (gm)
parsley	1/2 cup	8,000	.057	—	70	23	15	9.6	20
parsnips (6)	1/2 cup	100	.120	—	40	60	76	1.7	2
peaches, wht #	3 halves	100	.025	.065	6	10	19	0.2	1
peaches, yel #	1 lrg	1,000	.025	.065	9	10	19	0.3	1
pear	1 med.	17	.030	.060	4	15	18	0.3	0
peas, fresh*	1/2 cup	1,500	.390	.250	20	28	127	0.2	7
persimmon (7)	1 lrg	1,600	—	—	40	22	21	0.2	2
pineapple @	2/3 cup	30	.100	.025	38	8	26	0.2	0
plums	3 med.	130	.120	.056	5	20	27	0.5	1
potato, swt	1 med.	3,600	.155	.150	25	19	45	0.9	3
potato, wht	1 med.	0	.220	.075	33	13	53	1.5	3
potato, yam	1 med.	5,000	.180	.360	6	44	50	1.1	2
pumpkin	1/2 cup	2,500	.056	.057	8	23	50	0.9	1
radishes	15 lg	0	.030	.054	25	21	29	0.9	1
raspberries	1/2 cup	260	.021	—	30	41	38	0.8	1
rutabaga	3/4 cup	25	.075	.120	26	74	56	0.7	1
spinach*	1/2 cup	11,000	.090	.312	30	78	46	2.5	2
squash, hubd	1/2 cup	4,000	.050	.075	3	19	15	0.5	1
squash, sum.	1/2 cup	1,000	.040	.050	3	18	15	0.3	1
strawberries	1/2 cup	100	.025	—	50	34	28	0.6	1
tangerine	2 med.	300	.120	.054	48	42	17	0.2	1
tofu bean cake	120 grams	0	.070	.010	0	150	150	2.3	86
tomatoes	1 med.	1,500	.100	.050	25	11	29	0.4	1
turnips*	1/2 cup	0	.062	.062	22	56	47	0.5	1
turnip grns	1/2 cup	11,000	.060	.045	130	347	49	3.4	2
watercress	3/4 cup	1,250	.030	.090	15	40	11	0.8	0
watermelon	1 med sl	450	.180	.084	22	33	9	0.6	0

Legend: (1) inside white leaves; (2) outside green leaves; (3) Chinese; (4) diced; (5) bleached; (6) domestic; (7) Japanese; # pitted; * cooked; @ fresh
Modified from *International Turtle and Tortoise Society Journal*, August/September/October, 1970, and **Composition of Foods**, U.S. Department of Agriculture Handbook Number 8, Washington, DC, 1963.

on your pet. Wilted greens are satisfactory, however, and can be freshened by soaking in cool water for five or ten minutes. To help greens stay fresh longer, remove ties or rubber bands and fading leaves, rinse them, then roll them up jelly-roll style in a dishcloth. Store them in a plastic bag, leaving the end open, in the refrigerator.

In the past, my iguanas regularly ate boiled, free-range eggs, whole adult mice (or their parts), and more dog or monkey chow than was healthy. Fortunately, they were fed plenty of choice greens, vegetables and fruit, and always had fresh drinking water. In recent years, the near elimination of animal foods and increase in fiber and foliage has had a noticeable effect on the lizards and so, presumedly, has improved their health.

LOSS OF APPETITE/REFUSAL TO FEED

There are many reasons why any animal exhibits anorexia (the proper term to describe a lack of appetite or failure to feed): infectious or metabolic disease; parasitism; failure of the animal to adapt to the conditions of captivity; improper environmental temperature; too frequent handling and, of course, the wrong diet being offered.

Although the most common reason for anorexia is an inadequate or incorrect diet, environmental temperature also plays a major role. An environmental temperature which is too low to allow for normal activity of digestive enzymes will prevent even the well adapted reptile from displaying an appetite or from digesting or assimilating its food. Most reptiles exhibit active feeding when the environmental temperatures are approximately 25°–33° C (77°–91° F). Of course, exceptions exist within the iguanas.

Sometimes iguanas will refuse to feed just prior to or during their periodic skin shedding.

Often a brief exposure to natural *unfiltered* sunlight (not through a window pane) outdoors together with a "shower" will induce many previously anorectic iguanas to feed voluntarily.

A word of caution: Reptiles which have never exhibited overt aggression toward their keeper may display marked changes in behavior after even brief exposure to natural sunlight outdoors. This aggressiveness usually subsides as soon as the reptile is taken back to its enclosure. Many previously docile animals actually bite their owners who have been unwary enough to casually pick them up after they have been permitted to sunbathe. Nevertheless, sunbathing is highly therapeutic for iguanas. (This will be discussed further.) When given a choice between artificial basking lights and a splash of unfiltered sunlight, iguanas have been observed to opt for the sunshine consistently.

Some iguanas are often intolerant of handling after capture or after their familiar cages have been changed. These lizards should be left undisturbed after they have been moved to new quarters. A well-placed stout branch to climb and a hiding box or other refuge often prove useful in aiding the new captive chuckawalla, spiny-tailed, ground, and rock iguana to accept captivity and encourages it to commence feeding.

Reptiles are functionally "ectothermic," i.e., their body temperature is largely dependent upon the environmental temperature. Because of this, their basal metabolic rate usually is much lower than that of a similar size bird or mammal. Due to their lower rate of metabolism, reptiles can usually survive prolonged periods of fasting, but once they have crossed a poorly defined threshold, they decline in health very rapidly. At first, the affected animal lives off its stored fat, but soon this source of energy is exhausted and other tissues, especially muscle, are sacrificed to maintain life. The reptile slowly becomes gaunt and wasted and is more prone to infectious diseases and the stress of captivity.

As a rule, if an iguana or chuckawalla refuses to feed for a period of two weeks, its general health and the conditions under which it is being kept should be evaluated. If no physical evidence of disease is found, one or more hand-feedings should be given. The technique for this maneuver is provided below.

FORCED FEEDING

The lizard is restrained so that its head and body are supported. If necessary, the limbs are held closely against its body to keep the lizard from scratching the handler. Wrapping the lizard in a towel may help restrict its activity. The dewlap can be gently pulled downward as the head is supported, thus causing the lower jaw to descend; alternatively, the mouth can be opened gently with a clean soft rubber or plastic kitchen spatula. In very small lizards, a round wooden stick, such as those used for cotton-tipped swabs, can be rolled toward the back of the mouth, thus causing the jaw to open. If the dewlap is pulled downward, it must be done without great force to avoid tearing the soft tissue or fracturing the jaw. The food item (dandelion blossom, rolled tender leaves, softened alfalfa pellets, etc.) is placed into the mouth. The food is gradually and *gently* advanced into the back of the mouth and thence into the throat. A clean rubber eraser-tipped pencil can be used as a push rod to aid in passing the food down the esophagus until the meal is well down the lizard's body. Figure 17 a–d illustrates techniques for forced feeding.

A wide variety of invertebrates are also consumed by terrestrial iguanas. Spiders, silk-moth larvae, snails*, and earthworms are examples of species that are nutritious and easily captured or purchased. Other species such as crickets, mealworms and waxworms are less suitable due to their high phosphorus:low calcium contents and heavy cuticular exoskeletons. See Frye, 1991 a & b.

On pages 42–43 is a TABLE OF FOOD VALUES. Of particular interest is the ratio between the calcium and phosphorus values of certain food items. In order to maximize the nutritive value of a captive diet, the reader should compare these two mineral components. For example, compare

---

*Because snails often serve as the intermediate hosts for fluke parasites, only snails which have not been exposed to iguana feces should be used as food. Generally, flukes are rather host-specific and, thus, should not prove to be a hazard unless they have had access to the wastes of lizards or other reptiles.

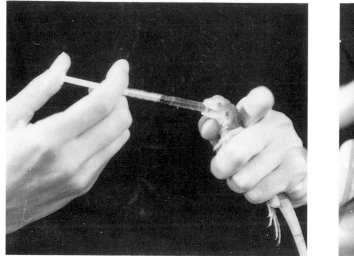
a

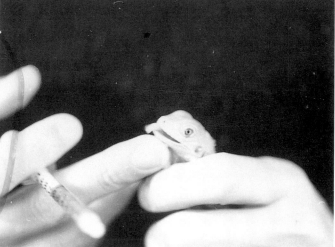
b

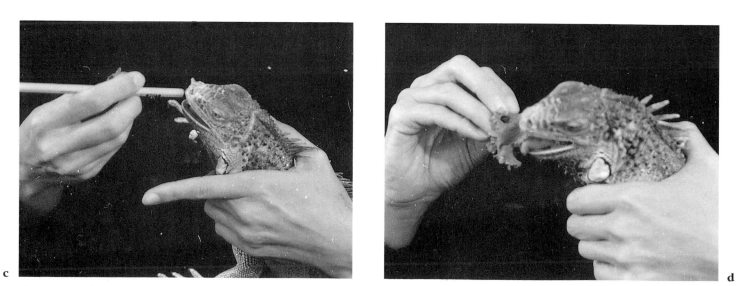
c

d

Figure 17 a–d. Sometimes forced feeding is necessary in order to accomplish short-term ingestion of nutrients. Liquid gruels are delivered into the mouth with a small syringe. Solid food items are placed into the mouth and, if necessary, are directed into the throat with a smooth round-ended pencil or other object. Photos by W. Townsend.

broccoli leaves, cabbage, collards, dandelion greens, endive, kale, mustard greens, and turnip greens which contain ample calcium and relatively low phosphorus, with such low calcium, high phosphorus items as apple, banana, cucumber, corn on the cob, grapes, iceberg lettuce, mushrooms, peas, peaches, plums, and Brussel's sprouts. Because the stiff stem-like leaf veins of some of these leafy varieties are fibrous, they should either be eliminated by trimming the leaves, or cut into short bite-size lengths before feeding to iguanas. Additional high-quality protein can be added to the nutritional ration by feeding legumes, especially pea and bean products. Tofu soybean cake is readily accepted by many iguanas.

The means for producing both nutritive grasses and various bean, pea, lentil, and pulse sprouts are presented in the next section.

Some potential food plants are toxic; the major ornamental plant species which contain toxic substances are listed in Table 3.

HYDROPONIC CULTIVATION OF GRASSES

With currently available hydroponic technology, high quality grasses can be readily produced in a limited space, without regard for climatic conditions and without the need for soil.

Several zoological gardens feed diets made from one or more hydroponically cultivated grasses (usually barley, wheat, oats and/or triticale) to their herbivorous animals. This technique has several distinct advantages over obtaining fresh green fodders from outside vendors: the initial capital expenditure is usually within the budgetary limits of most professional collections; the labor expenses required to seed, care for, and harvest each crop are modest; the quality and quantity of the grasses can be easily monitored and controlled; the quantity can be increased or decreased with little effort; the time required from seeding to harvest is quite brief, measuring only about one week; and the produce is pesticide and parasite free. The compact hydroponic growing units offer an opportunity to assure an economical and consistent supply of nutritious, highly palatable green feed.

Production models of these self-contained growing environments are, apparently, no longer manufactured, but it is possible to design and construct suitable units from off-the-shelf materials available at most building construction suppliers. One needs to provide a relatively closed environment in which the humidity and temperature can be controlled; an automatic illumination system employing fluorescent lighting of an appropriate wave length (examples are Sylvania Gro-Lux F20T-12/GRO, 20 watt,

61 cm; Sylvania Gro-Lux F40/GRO, 40 watt, 122 cm; Westinghouse Agrolite F20T12/AGRO, 20 watt, 61 cm; and Westinghouse Econ-O-Watt F40CW/RS/ EW-II, 34 watt); growing trays in which seeds can be sown; and an automatic time-controlled submersible pump to distribute the growing medium. A rack arrangement is used to suspend the growing trays. Two or three times a day, the pump distributes a balanced growing solution to the growing trays; these trays are self-emptying through overflow standpipes so that they cannot overflow. After the pumps are turned off, any surplus growth medium is returned to a sump or other suitable container in which the pump is submersed. The photoperiod is controlled by a time clock which activates the light sources several times a day.

Smaller earthless growing units are available from some nursery dealers, or they can be made at home. One can construct several experimental models using a large-diameter polyvinylchloride irrigation pipe split lengthwise to hold pea gravel-sized tumbled volcanic pumice, and small submersible pumps to circulate the growth medium. These experimental units have some advantages over some of the commercially produced models and are substantially less expensive.

The amateur herpetologist or professional who has a relatively small collection may wish to build a small pilot model in which a more modest amount of fresh food can be grown. An excellent source of information, plans, and growing supplies is Hydro-Fresh Farm, P.O. Box 511, San Martin, CA 95046. The balanced growth medium is available from this firm. In addition, local, state, and federal agricultural extension offices should be consulted for details of the various processes and/or plans. Small quantities of green feed can be produced in jars. (See next section.)

BEAN, PEA, LENTIL, AND SEED SPROUT CULTURE

Home-sprouted seeds and pulses (peas, beans, lentils, etc.) are excellent sources for macro- and micronutrients in diets for herbivorous reptiles. The ease of producing these sprouts in varying quantities and the low cost of equipment and seed stock make the culture of these nutritious and desirable items attractive for the reptile collections of large institutions as well as more modest private amateur hobbyist collections. Furthermore, these sprouts are appropriate for human consumption.

The following pulses are particularly appropriate for sprouting: small mung beans, adzuki beans, garbanzo beans (chickpeas), whole green or yellow peas, and lentils. The following seeds are well suited for sprouting: soft wheat berries, triticale, maize, whole unsalted sunflower seeds, millet, rapeseed, alfalfa, and barley. Small quantities of radish seeds may be added to mixtures to enhance the excellent flavor of the resulting young sprouts. Radish sprouts impart a tangy flavor and are readily accepted by reptiles; however, too many make the entire sprout crop too spicy for most animals (and humans).

All beans, peas, lentils, and seeds must be obtained from sources intended for human consumption, such as health food stores. Sprouted seeds and pulses sold for garden or farm use must not be fed to animals or consumed by humans because they are often treated with fungicides and insecticides that are highly toxic.

The only equipment required to produce small quantities of fresh sprouts are 1 quart or larger glass canning jars fitted with outer rings holding disks of fiberglass or stainless steel screening mesh. Larger volumes of sprouts require correspondingly larger containers.

To induce sprouting, 1½ to 2 tablespoons of dry mixed seeds and pulses are placed into the container, and slightly tepid tap water is added to cover the seeds to a depth of approximately 10 cm (4 inches). The seeds are allowed to soak overnight. As they soak, they absorb water and often swell to twice their original size. After approximately 12 hours of soaking, the water is poured off through the screened lid and the now softened mixture of seeds is allowed to germinate in a dark area. After approximately 36 hours, the first tiny sprouts appear. Each day, rinse the jars of sprouting seeds and pulses in cold water and thoroughly drain them through the screened lid. After three to five days, the sprouts are ready to harvest. At that time, rinse the sprouts in cold water, remove them from the jars, and use them immediately or store them in a refrigerator. Culturing the sprouts in total darkness is particularly important if some of them are to be consumed by humans because, as the sprouts mature, they develop chlorophyll which may impart a bitter flavor to the now green sprouts. Although this flavor may be objectionable to humans, it does not appear to affect the palatability to herbivorous reptiles and, in fact, actually improves the nutritional value of the sprouts.

Depending upon the varieties and quantities grown, a few cents' worth of dry seeds and pulses provide over a liter of fresh sprouts in as few as four days, and they may be produced every month of the year. Pulses and alfalfa are excellent sources of high-quality vegetable protein, vitamins, minerals (including calcium), and useful energy in the form of cellulose and other complex carbohydrates.

Fresh sprouts are especially valuable for treating tortoises and iguanas that have become accustomed to eating only iceberg lettuce, cabbage, or other nutritionally deficient vegetable items. The sprouts should be sprinkled as a top dressing over the animal's preferred leafy items so that the animal must eat its way through the sprouts in order to reach the lettuce or cabbage, thus ingesting both its preferred items and those more nutritionally sound items placed in its gustatorial pathway. At each daily feeding, the proportion of sprouts is increased in relation to that of the lettuce or cabbage. Dandelions, nasturtiums, grasses, rose petals, etc., can also be placed in the reptile's field of vision. Usually within two weeks or less, the animal may be sufficiently retrained to accept a far more nutritional and varied vegetable diet. Sprouts also are a superb means of increasing the caloric and other nutritional factors of a ration designed to promote rapid weight gain.

HIGH-FIBER DIET FOR HERBIVOROUS REPTILES

This diet is the result of years of Dr. Juli Sweet's experience with iguanine species, has proven to be nutritionally sound, and is well accepted by the animals to which it is fed. It is applicable for *Brachylophus*, *Conolophus*, *Ctenosaurus*, *Cyclura*, *Dipsosaurus*, *Iguana*, and *Sauromalus*. It is reproduced here with Dr. Sweet's permission:

Dr. Sweet's Diet

> natural wheat bran cereal
> alfalfa pellets
> 9-grain bread
> alfalfa sprouts
> clover sprouts
> natural honey
> Superpreen®-Blair's Products, RHB Laboratories, Inc. Available from Bush Herpetological Supply, 4869 S. Bradley Road, Suite 18B-180, Santa Maria, CA 93455, 1-800-676-4809
> vitamin B complex with folic acid
> purified water
> calcium carbonate powder

Equal portions of bran and alfalfa pellets are mixed with 0.5 kg of 9-grain bread and 0.25 kg each of alfalfa and clover sprouts. This mixture is moistened with 120 ml of honey and 720 ml of water. The dosage of Superpreen is approximately 12 mg per kg of body weight. Vitamin B complex supplement is added to the mixture at a rate that will yield a dosage of 50 mg/kg twice weekly. Calcium carbonate is administered at a rate of 200 mg/kg/week.

Dr. Sweet has raised several generations of iguanas on this diet in addition to mixed fruits and melons, mixed raw green and yellow/orange vegetables (yams, sweet potatoes, squash), grasses, legumes, flowers and buds (roses, dandelions, etc.), cactus pads, sprouted seeds, infant cereals, brown rice, cereal breads, and assorted cooked meats and eggs. She recommends that animal protein sources be fed only twice monthly. Immature lizards are fed ad lib, adults are fed three times weekly.

As mentioned earlier in this chapter, the gastrointestinal tract of most herbivorous reptiles is populated by a variety of symbiotic microorganisms. A näive herbivorous lizard should be fed gradually increasing amounts of concentrated diets for several weeks so that its intestinal microflora can become accustomed to a diet containing such complex carbohydrates as honey, cereal grains, and bread. Such an acclimatization period may require several weeks after a diet of mostly vegetables and fruit.

CHAPTER 3

TOXIC PLANT POISONING

There are many species of mildly irritating to profoundly toxic wild and cultivated plants that are occasionally ingested by captive reptiles. Table 4 is a partial list of the more common species that have been implicated in plant intoxications.

Ctenosaurus
similis

TABLE 4
Toxic Plants

Plant name	Toxic portion(s)
Acokanthera	Flowers and fruit
Aconite (monk's hood)	Roots, flowers, leaves and seeds
Amaryllis	Bulb, stem, flower parts
Amsinckia (Tarweed)	Foliage and seeds
Anemone	Leaves, flowers
Apple (seeds only)	Seeds (only if crushed)
Apricot (seeds only)	Inner seeds
Autumn crocus	Bulbs
Avocado	Foliage
Azalea	Foliage, flowers
Baneberry	Foliage, fruits
Beach pea	Foliage, peas, and pods
Betal nut palm	All parts
Belladonna	Berries and others parts
Bittersweet	Berries
Bird of paradise	Foliage, flowers, seed pods
Black locust	Bark, sprouts, and foliage
Bleeding heart	Foliage, flowers, and roots
Bloodroot	All parts
Bluebonnet	Foliage and flowers
Bottlebrush	Flower parts
Boxwood	Foliage and twigs
Buckeye horse chestnut	Sprouts and nuts
Buttercup	All parts
Caladium	All parts
Calla lily	All parts
Cardinal flower	All parts
Carolina jessamine	Foliage, flowers, and sap
Casava	Roots
Castor bean	Uncooked beans
Chalice or trumpet vine	All parts
Cherry (inner seeds only)	Inner pit seeds
Cherry laurel	Foliage and flowers
China berry tree	Berries
Christmas berry	Berries
Christmas cactus (*Euphorbia*)	Entire plant
Christmas rose	Foliage and flowers
Columbine	Foliage, flowers, seeds
Common privet	Foliage and berries
Coral plant	All parts
Crocus	Bulbs
Croton	Foliage, shoots
Cyclamen	Foliage, stems, and flowers
Daffodil	Bulbs, foliage, flowers, and pods
Daphne	Berries
Death camus	All parts are toxic; esp. roots
Deadly nightshade	Foliage, unripe fruit, sprouts

TABLE 4
Toxic Plants (continued)

Plant name	Toxic portion(s)
Delphinium	Bulbs, foliage, flowers and seeds
Destroying angel (death cap)	All parts of the mushroom
Dogwood	Fruit mildly toxic
Dumb cane (*Dieffenbachia*)	Foliage
Eggplant	Foliage only
Elderberry	Leaves, bark, and shoots
Elephant ear (taro)	Foliage
English ivy	Esp. berries
Euphorbia (spurge(s))	Foliage, flowers, latex-like sap
False hellebore	All parts
Fiddleneck (*Senecio*)	All parts
Fly agaric (amanita, deathcap)	All parts (cap and stem)
Four o'clock	All parts
Foxglove	Foliage and flowers
Gelsemium	All parts
Golden chain	Seeds and pods
Hemlock roots (water & poison)	All parts
Henbane	All parts
Holly, English and American	Foliage and berries
Horse chestnut	All parts
Horsetail reed (*Equisetum*)	All parts
Hyacinth	Bulbs, foliage and flowers
Hydrangea	All parts
Impatiens (touch-me-not)	All parts
Iris (flags)	Bulbs and roots, foliage and flowers
Ivy (all forms)	Foliage and fruit
Jack-in-the-pulpit	Roots are mildly toxic
Jasmine	Foliage and flowers, esp. nectar
Jamine, star	Foliage, flowers
Jatropha	Seeds and oily sap
Jerusalem cherry	Foliage and fruit
Jessamine	Berries
Jimson weed (thorn apple)	Foliage, flowers and pods
Johnson grass, wilted	All parts
Lambkill (sheep laurel)	Foliage
Lantana camara	Foliage, flowers, and esp. berries
Larkspur	Entire young plant; seeds & pods
Laurel	All parts
Lily of the valley	Foliage and flowers
Lobelia	All parts
Locoweed	All parts
Locust(s)	All parts
Lupine	Esp. seeds and pods, foliage
Machineel	All parts
Marijuana	All parts
May apple	Fruit
Mescal	All parts may be toxic

TABLE 4
Toxic Plants (continued)

Plant name	Toxic portion(s)
Milk weed	Foliage
Mistletoe	Foliage and berries
Moccasin flower	Foliage and flowers
Monkshood	Entire plant, including roots
Moonseed	Berries
Morning glory	Foliage, flowers, and seeds
Mountain laurel	Young leaves and shoots
Mushrooms (some wild forms)	Entire cap and stem
Narcissus	Bulb, flowers
Natal cherry	Berries, foliage
Nectarine (inner seed only)	Only inner pit seeds
Nicotine, tree, bush, flowering	Foliage and flowers
Nightshades	All parts, esp. unripe fruits
Oak trees	Leaves and acorns
Oleander	Foliage, stems, and flowers
Peach (inner seed only)	Inner pit seeds
Pear (seeds only)	Seeds (only if crushed)
Pennyroyal	Foliage and flowers
Peony	Foliage and flowers
Periwinkle	All parts
Philodendrons, some species	All parts
Pinks	All parts
Plum (seeds only)	Inner seeds; foliage can be toxic
Poinsettia	Foliage, flowers and latex sap
Poison hemlock	Foliage and seeds
Poison ivy	Foliage and fruit
Poison oak	Foliage and fruit
Poison sumac	Foliage and fruit
Pokewood or pokeberry	Roots, fruit
Poppy (except California)	All parts
Potato	Raw foliage and sprouts ("eyes")
Privet	Berries, foliage
Redwood	Resinoids leached when wood is wet
Rhubarb	Uncooked foliage and stems
Rhododendron	Foliage and flowers
Rosary pea	Foliage, flowers and peapods
Rosemary	Foliage in some species
Russian thistle	Foliage and flowering parts
Sage	Foliage in some species
Salmonberry	Foliage and fruit
Scarlet pimpernel	Foliage, flowers and fruit
Scotch broom	Seeds
Senecio ("fiddle neck")	All parts
Skunk cabbage	Roots
Snapdragon	Foliage and flowers
Spanish bayonet	Foliage and flowers
Squirrel corn	Foliage, flowering parts, and seeds

TABLE 4
Toxic Plants (continued)

Plant name	Toxic portion(s)
Sudan grass, wilted	All parts
Star of Bethlehem	Foliage and flowering parts
Sundew	Foliage
Sweetpea	Stems
Tansy	Foliage and flowers
Taro (elephant ears)	Foliage
Tarweed	Foliage and seeds
Tiger lily	Foliage, flowers, and seed pods
Toad flax	Foliage
Tomato plant	Foliage and vines
Toyon berry	Berries
Tree of heaven	Foliage and flowering parts
Trillium	Foliage
Trumpet vine	All parts
Tulip	Bulb, foliage, and flowering parts
Venus flytrap	Foliage and funnel flowering parts
Verbena	Foliage and flowers
Vetch (several forms)	Seeds and pods
Virginia creeper	Foliage and seed pods
Water hemlock	Roots and foliage
Wild parsnip	Underground roots and foliage
Wisteria	Foliage, seeds, and pods
Yellow star thistle	Foliage and flowering parts
Yew	Foliage

Modified from a list compiled by the *International Turtle and Tortoise Journal* May-June, 1969, a compilation by the San Diego Poison Information Center, University of California, San Diego, and the San Diego Turtle and Tortoise Society, published in the *Tortuga Gazette* January, 1982. Also see Garner, 1961; Hulbert & Oehme, 1961; Tucker & Kimball, 1961; and U.S. Dept. of Agriculture, 1958.

Iguana Iguana

CHAPTER 4

REPRODUCTION

A major goal of many people who keep iguanas in captivity is to induce these lizards to reproduce. Climatic conditions often prevent housing these animals outdoors in simulated natural habitats. However, significant advances have been made in providing indoor quarters that meet the many environmental requirements for these tropical iguanas. The greatest progress has been with the captive breeding of *Iguana iguana*, *Cyclura cornuta*, *C. nubila*, *C. ricordi*, and *Brachylophus faciatus*.

Incubation and productive hatching of iguana eggs is one thing; providing an acceptable environment and social milieu that encourages successful mating is another. Observations of wild populations of green iguanas have yielded information that suggests that virtually all courtship and copulation occurs within defined territories. These territorial prerogatives are essential to a male's reproductive success. Moreover, the subtleties of courtship are an important factor in female mate choice and in facilitating a female's receptivity (Burghardt, 1978; Rand, 1978). Sometimes, the presence of a competing male exerts a stimulatory effect upon an otherwise sluggish male with a flagging libido. Similarly, more than one female kept with a solitary male often serves as a stimulant to courtship. This may be due to an augmentation of pheromonal scent cues within a given space. Additionally, exposure to unfiltered sunlight and a light shower also are stimulants to courtship activity. At any rate, the male must be perceived as fit by any prospective female before she will accept his advances. Exceptions to this situation usually involve opportunistic matings by smaller and persistent males. It is for this reason that many large male iguanas exhibit such hostility towards their smaller cage mates (of questionable gender). Combat between competing males is relatively common when more than a single male occupies a delineated territory, but these combative encounters are only rarely fatal, usually amounting to miscellaneous bites on or about the head, neck, and forelimbs. Deposed

59

males should be removed from the confines of a dominant male's territory because the constant harassment will lead to its decline in health and fitness, starvation, and death.

Most iguanas reach sexual maturity between their third and fourth years; the smaller forms may achieve sexual maturity as early as the second year; and the large rhinoceros iguanas might not become mature before their seventh or eighth year, depending upon nutritional, environmental, and husbandry conditions. Even very small sexually mature males may try to copulate with much larger females (Figure 18).

Figure 18—see page 87

Sexually mature male green iguanas, especially those housed with one or more females, tend to feed sparsely during mating season which, depending upon geographical latitude, runs from October through April. During courtship and later, while the fertilized eggs are maturing and receiving their shells, females may cease eating altogether. This activity usually follows two to three and one-half months after copulation. Because egg production is a stressful process for the females, they should be healthy and possess excellent flesh prior to and during the mating season.

Each member of these species displays its stereotypical courtship rituals and, if two or more males are involved, they may go through mock battle with each other, with the winner claiming the female as his prize. Mating is accomplished by the apposition of the male's cloaca with that of the receptive female, and the insertion of one hemipenis into her cloacal vent. In order to help him maneuver his mate, the male iguana grasps the female near her shoulders with his teeth (Figure 19); as a result, mated females often display skin wounds that bear mute witness to their amorous adventures (Figure 20 a & b).

Figure 19—see page 87

Figure 20 a–b—see page 88

Interestingly, the mere presence of a male can induce egg formation and deposition in a female whether or not successful copulation has occurred. Females containing eggs, whether they are fertile or infertile, display obvious abdominal swelling, commence searching for a suitable nesting site, then begin excavating the substrate in the site with all four limbs before gravidity is evident to the observer. Within a week that this behavior is first observed, a nesting box should be provided so that the lizard will remain at ease, secure, and will accept the nesting material as a suitable site for depositing her eggs. Medium-sized dog houses which have a hinged or removable roof make excellent nesting boxes. The interior of the box is treated with polyurethane varnish and permitted to outgas (as described in the **HOUSING** section of this text). A board approximately 30 cm (12 inches) should be affixed across the entrance, making certain that there are no protruding nails that could injure the occupants. The inside of the container is filled with a mixture of clean, slightly moistened sand and sphagnum moss. Although the eggs will be incubated in another container, ideally the nesting box should be placed in a warm corner of the enclosure because this makes the nesting site more attractive to the female lizards. The incubation medium should be damp, but never soggy. The nesting temperatures for several species of iguanas is provided in Table 5. These temperatures should not fluctuate more than approximately +/− 1–2° C from those printed in Table 5.

Occasionally, the eggs are resorbed before they can be laid. This is a natural means for the recycling of vital protein, fat-laden yolk, and calcium, but sometimes the eggs become necrotic and the female becomes intoxicated by the products of the eggs' decomposition.

Actual egg laying, or *oviposition*, can require as much as three days to complete, after which the female will appear thin. Usually, she will commence eating regularly and will regain her lost weight within a few weeks. If a female appears to be weak or depressed, she should be examined and her condition evaluated by a veterinarian, and corrective action taken. The most common complication of egg laying is obstruction of one or both of the oviducts through which the shelled eggs must pass. As the eggs pass down these tubular organs, they receive their lightly calcified shells from specialized glands lining the hollow oviducts. Before the female deposits her clutch, the swelling of her belly can be substantial and the outline of several eggs can often be seen easily. Interestingly, many female reptiles can store living sperm in their reproductive tracts and use them to fertilize other clutches of eggs several years after their last contact with a fertile male; this process is called *amphigonia retardata*. Overly large, misshapen, or decomposed eggs with abnormal shells, infection, or low blood calcium levels are conditions which require immediate veterinary care.

The diagnosis of pregnancy (or, more properly, gravidity) in iguanas is relatively easy because the eggs can be seen as bulges within the abdominal cavity (Figure 21) These eggs, which are still in the oviducts, can be felt by gently passing your fingertips over them as you stroke the lizard's flanks, just behind her ribcage. The eggs are relatively soft shelled (Figure 22) and can be damaged by rough handling.

Incubation and embryonic development are triggered by exposure to air. It is for this reason that even if an iguana carries her fertilized eggs for a prolonged period, they will not develop until they have been deposited in appropriate nesting material such as dampened sphagnum moss, a mixture of moist sand and leaf mold, or other humus rich organic substance. Once deposited, the eggs should be transferred with a minimum of handling to a container of nesting medium. Incubation temperatures and gestation times are given in Table 5. The hatchling iguanas are miniature copies of their parents (shown earlier in Figure 5) and once having left the confines of their eggshells, they become fully independent.

Figure 21—see page 88

Figure 22—see page 88

Whether or not they are exposed to males of their own species, some female iguanas produce multiple clutches of eggs and, as a result of the progressive drain on their bodily economy, decline alarmingly in condition. These lizards can be spayed in a fashion much like that performed on dogs and cats (Figure 23). This surgical procedure can often greatly prolong the life of a pet iguana, and should be discussed with your veterinarian if you are not interested in propagating the species in your home. The operation is performed under a general anesthetic and employs sterile surgical techniques. Under the correct conditions, it is safe and highly efficacious. Interestingly, spayed iguanas tend to live longer than intact females. This is probably a reflection of the enormous metabolic drain imposed during the egg formation and laying processes. The mere production of shelled eggs requires an immense amount of fat, protein, and calcium—all of which must be mobilized and drawn from stores in the female's body tissues. The formation of eggs also is an intensive demand on available energy for which the gravid female iguana must compensate by increasing her intake of high-quality, nutritious food. In addition to proper nutrition, the gravid female iguana must always have a supply of fresh drinking water available in the form of droplets sprayed on edible foliage. During the latter stages of intraoviductal egg development, most female iguanas reduce their food intake markedly or even refuse to feed altogether. This behavior is entirely normal and only reflects the diminshed volume in the coelomic cavity caused by the mass of eggs that now occupies most of the available space. Usually, female iguanas resume feeding soon after depositing their eggs.

Figure 23—see page 89

Miscellaneous Considerations

Iguanas of several species may display what can only be described as homosexual behavior. Although both males and females have been observed in pseudocopulation with members of the same sex, this is not considered abnormal behavior by these animals, and may only represent one form of a display of social dominance (see Köhler, 1991 a & b).

TABLE 5
Significant Egg and Incubation Data

Species	Time from mating to oviposition (days)	Clutch size (#)	Average egg dimensions (cm)	Average egg weight (gm)	Incubation temp (°C)	Incubation time (days)	Hatchability (%)	Reference
Brachylophus faciatus	?	2–8	21 × 40	10	24–27	163	50	1
						164		
						184		
Iguana iguana	65	10–53	15.4	?	28–32	59–85	46–88	2
						65		
					26–33		56–71	2
		49						4
		48						5
		86						3
Cyclura cornuta	?	10	40.8 × 83		28–29	72–83		8
			43.4 × 66.7		26.5	100		6
					29.5	85		7
Cyclura nubila	?	17	44.5 × 65.6					6

References: 1 Arnett, 1979; 2 Banks, 1984; 3 Boylan, 1963; 4 Hirth, 1963; 5 Mendelssohn, 1980; 6 Shaw, 1954; 7 Shaw, 1969; 8 Tonge & Bloxam, 1984

Conolophus subcristatus

CHAPTER 5

DISORDERS RELATED TO THE ALIMENTARY SYSTEM

NUTRITIONAL DISORDERS

Although iguanas are prone to several infectious, and parasitic diseases, and metabolic disorders, they are usually hardy in captivity if their environment and care are appropriate, and may live for nearly twenty years or more in exceptional cases. The most common illnesses encountered in captive iguanas of all species are related to nutrition. These difficulties may reflect gross malnutrition originating from insufficient food, or deficient quality of the foodstuffs that are fed; generally, it is the latter condition that induces disease.

Growing iguanas require a well balanced diet that contains adequate calcium without a concomitant oversufficiency of phosphorus. The reasons for this are highly technical, but suffice it to state here that when a diet too rich in phosphorus is fed, even including sufficient calcium-rich food items may be inadequate to prevent a shift in the amounts of calcium and phosphorus in the blood plasma.

Metabolic Bone Disease

Once such an imbalance of calcium and phosphorus occurs, tiny glands in the lizard's neck are stimulated to secrete a hormone that causes calcium stored in the bones to be removed and lost from the urine. If this loss is not controlled and the calcium that was lost is not replaced, the result is a condition called *metabolic bone disease*. The early signs of this disorder are gradual swelling of limbs and, particularly, jaw bones, which may become markedly shortened (Figure 24 a–e). What at first may appear to

Figure 24 a–e—see pages 89 & 90

be chubby limbs really are severely softened bones and wasted muscle tissue. In extreme cases, muscular twitching, spasms, and paralysis can occur.

Metabolic bone disease usually can be linked to diets consisting of head lettuce, grapes, bananas and other fruit, mealworms, crickets, and greens such as spinach. Each of these items is rich in available phosphorus, but very deficient in calcium. In addition, spinach contains a substance, oxalic acid, which reacts with calcium and forms an insoluble salt, calcium oxalate. Not only will calcium be lost to the lizard's bones, but the calcium oxalate can damage the kidneys severely enough to cause uremia.

The information given in the section on nutrition and the Table of Food Values (Table 3) will help you select those foods that are rich in calcium and other essential nutrients. Moreover, they are palatable to the lizards. Since lizards can perceive colors, especially red, orange, yellow, and green, one should select those food items that are visually attractive, as well as flavorful.

Rickets

Rickets is another form of metabolic bone disease characterized by softening of the bones. In this disease, the available dietary calcium may be sufficient, but there is a dietary or environmental deficiency of vitamin D. Either the preformed molecule is not present in the food, or the animal is not exposed to suitable ultraviolet irradiation. The end result is identical in that the calcium is not absorbed from the intestine.

Rather than forming bone substance by the orderly mineralization of cartilage "templates" at the ends of growing bones, the bones of lizards suffering from rickets tend to undergo a variable degree of cartilage overgrowth called hypertrophy (abnormally large cell *size*) and hyperplasia (abnormally large *numbers* of cells). Such bones remain very poorly mineralized and, thus, are soft. One characteristic of this disorder is the formation of swellings termed "rachitic rosettes" at the junctions where the ribs that join the breastbone meet those that articulate with the vertebrae. These structures are rounded swellings that can be seen as the lizard's ribcage expands during each breath. In addition, the ends of the limb bones may be greatly thickened, or buttressed. The ends of the bones next to adjacent joints become broadly flared.

X-ray photographs, called *radiographs*, of affected bones reveal little or no evidence of mineralization. The outer layers of bone also exhibit marked thinning. Fractures also are frequently seen, particularly in weight-bearing limb bones as well as ribs and vertebrae.

The other side of this problem is a diet overly rich in vitamin D and calcium. Some references advise feeding dog or cat food or monkey biscuits to iguanas. Indeed, many iguanas eagerly eat these rations, but the major difficulty with feeding them is that they were formulated for dogs, cats, or monkeys, not herbivorous iguanas. Vitamin D is required by animals to aid in the absorption of calcium from the digested food in the large intestine. The problem is that with too much vitamin D, there is an overabsorption of calcium. This abnormally high plasma calcium level results in the deposition of calcium in tissues in which it is not normally found. These sites can be heart muscle, blood vessels, lung, spleen, liver, brain, skeletal muscle, and skin. One can easily imagine that these normally soft and pliant tissues would be impaired in their important functions if they become severely mineralized.

Fortunately, an effective treatment for too much calcium in the blood plasma and soft tissues, called *hypercalcemia*, has been developed (Frye, 1991 b; Frye and Centofanti, 1991) and the deleterious effects of this condition can be reversed. It requires that the iguana be treated in a veterinary hospital for about two weeks. Since this is an entirely preventable disorder, attention to what you feed your iguana is necessary.

Vitamin Deficiencies and Excesses

Vitamin A deficiency is extremely rare in iguanas because their diet usually consists of vegetables which contain ample amounts of beta carotene, the metabolic precursor of vitamin A. Present in both green leafy plants and yellow and orange vegetables and fruits, beta carotene is converted in the digestive process to one or more forms of vitamin A. Diets rich in animal protein can deplete stores of vitamin A in the liver. The signs of vitamin A deficiency usually are referable to the eyes and respiratory system. Swollen or reddened eyelids and their associated mucous membranes, nasal discharges or respiratory distress are typical, but remember that vitamin A deficiency in an herbivore is extremely rare and should be thoroughly investigated before administering injectable or even oral vitamin A supplements.

A condition of vitamin A overdosage sometimes occurs as a result of the administration of excessive amounts of injectable vitamin A in the hope of stimulating a flagging diet. There is no evidence that vitamin A has a salutory effect on a poor appetite, and its use for this purpose should be discontinued.

Thiamin

Thiamin (Vitamin B$_1$) deficiency is not caused by feeding a thiamin-deficient diet per se but, rather, a diet which contains an enzyme that destroys thiamin already in the lizard's body tissues. Some plants, particularly some ferns and other ornamental house plants, contain this enzyme, *thiaminase*. The signs of thiamin deficiency consist of nerve disorders, inability to use certain muscle groups, twitching, and muscular spasms. Similar muscular abnormalities can be seen in vitamin E and/or selenium deficiency.

Discovered early and treated with oral or injectable thiamin hydrochloride, this vitamin deficiency almost always can be treated effectively. Again, prevention is preferable to treatment.

Other B-Complex Vitamins and Vitamin C

Deficiencies in the other B complex vitamins are unusual in iguanas because they are synthesized in the intestinal tract by the normal intestinal flora composed of beneficial bacteria and protozoa that reside in these animals. Under some circumstances, these microorganisms are killed off by antibiotics; then the entire digestive process becomes impaired and vitamin deficiencies can occur. Similarly, vitamin C is produced by specialized cells within the kidney and gastrointestinal tract. A deficiency of vitamin C is highly unusual in iguanas. Its signs would include bleeding gums, particularly after the normal shedding of teeth which occurs sporadically throughout the lizard's life; bruising; and other nonspecific clinical manifestations.

Vitamin D

We have already discussed vitamin D and its role in calcium. When deficient, calcium is not absorbed from the large intestine in sufficient amounts to support and maintain normal bone growth. When present in abnormally large amounts, too much calcium is absorbed and the excess is deposited in tissues that should not be mineralized.

Vitamin E and Selenium

Vitamin E deficiency can occur but, generally, only as a result of a grossly abnormal diet that is rich in rancid or saturated fatty acids. Since most iguanas kept as pets are largely herbivorous, such an abnormal diet is most unusual.

The micronutrient selenium can be both essential for growth and maintenance of normal tissues and, when present in excessive quantities, it can be toxic. It shares an important role with vitamin C, vitamin E, and, to a lesser extent, vitamin A, as an antioxidant. There are geographic locations throughout the world where soils in which edible plants are grown are deficient in selenium; conversely, in some areas under intense agriculture and irrigation which use subsurface water pumping, the levels of selenium salts in plants can be excessive and even toxic. If the vegetables you feed your iguana were grown in selenium-deficient soil, a small amount of supplemental selenium can be added to the ration. The amount necessary to maintain health is miniscule. Your veterinarian can aid you in deciding whether and/or how much supplement should be employed. The clinical signs of selenium deficiency are variable, but usually include some form of muscular dystrophy, including the heart muscle. Clinical signs may include muscle weakness, muscle tremors, fatigue, or sudden death. There may or may not be inflammation and gross alteration, especially hardening of body fat also.

Mineral Deficiencies or Imbalances

Iodine

Other micronutritional deficiencies can occur as a result of feeding abnormal diets to iguanas. An example is iodine, which usually is present in well balanced diets formulated for herbivores. However, if the diet is composed mostly of plants of the cabbage family, a deficiency of thyroid hormone can be induced because there are substances in these vegetables that inhibit the absorption of iodine—which is essential for the synthesis of thyroid hormone. A chronic deficiency in available iodine usually results in a change in the thyroid gland. The gland becomes enlarged and is called a "goiter." If the goitrous thyroid gland becomes sufficiently large, it may cause a noticeable swelling in the anterior portion of the chest cavity; more often, as the gland enlarges, it displaces other organs such as the heart or lungs, or may compress the esophagus and cause difficulty in swallowing. Other changes can be seen also, but are less consistent. When this condition is diagnosed by a veterinarian, most often with the assistance of thyroid function laboratory tests, the treatment is aimed at altering the diet so that fewer cabbage-like plants are fed and an additional source of iodine is included in the diet. This supplemental iodine can be added easily by feeding ground kelp tablets sprinkled as a top dressing on favored food items; ⅟₁₆ to ½ tablet/day, depending upon the size of the iguana given over a period of two weeks will treat this deficiency. Because kelp is not particularly toxic, even a small overdosage is harmless.

Sodium

Since all living animal tissues require sodium for their maintenance, and since sodium is so ubiquitous in most plants, there is seldom a necessity to add sodium chloride (table salt) to the captive diet. Iguanas possess an interesting and highly efficient means for handling the problem of excreting excess salt without having to lose precious water from their bodies. This last requirement is especially important when considering the dry desert habitats in which some iguanine lizards live. Specialized glandular structures whose secretory products empty into the nasal cavities are located just beneath the surface of the tissue lining the nasal passages. It is for this reason that iguanas sneeze frequently. This sneezing does not mean that your iguana has a "cold." Rather, it is an entirely normal behavior. You might notice that the fluid that these lizards sneeze out tends to form crusts around the nostrils and, if dried on clear glass or plastic surfaces, will form crystal-like white spots that were illustrated previously (Figure 14 b). **Figure 14 b—see page 34** These dried deposits consist of chloride salts of sodium and potassium. As the lizards burrow beneath the surface of their cage litter, these nasal deposits often are scraped off and lost. However, if the lizard is less active, the salt crystals may accumulate (Figure 14 a). **Figure 14 a—see page 87**

MISCELLANEOUS DISORDERS

Constipation and Gastrointestinal Blockages

The feces of captive reptiles vary widely in their consistency, content, and frequency. There are no specific guidelines with which to judge whether a particular animal is constipated. The digestive process depends substantially upon the food content, environmental temperature and, consequently, body temperature of the animal, and length of time since its last meal. The very nature of the food that is ingested plays a major role also; many small particles possess a greater surface area upon which digestive enzymes and juices can act than an identical weight represented as larger pieces. If water is not readily available to the lizard, the stool masses may become dry, thus impeding their passage through the intestines, particularly the colon where the majority of moisture absorption occurs.

Iguanas occasionally suffer from the inability to complete the passage of ingesta through the digestive tract. In captivity, exercise may be severely curtailed, diets may lack sufficient roughage, and some of the animals may ingest large amounts of cage litter, such as sand, gravel, ground corn cob, or wood chips. It is not uncommon for some captive reptiles to become grossly obese. All of these factors favor intestinal blockages and constipation, and must be avoided.

Treatment ranges from bathing the animal in tepid water (which often is sufficient to induce defecation) to major surgery for physically removing masses of dried stool and foreign material from the intestine.

Medical management of constipation often produces satisfactory resolution. Small amounts of petroleum jelly, magnesium oxide (milk of magnesia) suspension, or stool softening agents such as *dilute* dioctyl sodium sulfosuccinate (DSS), phenolphthalein, and/or stool bulk augmenters such as hemicellulose, may be sufficient. Siblin (Park-Davis) is an easily available medication. Several proprietary laxative products formulated for cats are highly effective, and are readily available from veterinarians. A small volume of any of these products is placed into the mouth of the affected iguana. Solid laxatives are less likely to be inhaled than liquid mineral oil and, therefore, are preferred by most veterinarians who treat iguanas.

Many herpetoculturists employ pelleted alfalfa rabbit or guinea pig chow as cage litter. When this material is purposefully or accidentally ingested, it provides essential nutrients and safe fiber. When swallowed, it soon softens and is digested. The non-nutritive fiber contributes to the stool bulk and is passed in the feces without inducing blockages. However, it ferments rapidly when moistened and soiled. Therefore, it should be changed frequently. One good means for providing both a toileting area and a supply of pelleted alfalfa is to place a pan or tray of the material into the cage and change it as it becomes moist or soiled with feces.

With the retention of fecal material in the large bowel, there is a progressive absorption of fluid from the stools. Soon, these boluses become abnormally dry and hard; normal peristaltic waves that propel the stools toward the rectum and anus can no longer move them. Radiography at this point may reveal a physiological blockage called an ileus, with gas-filled loops of intestine just in front of the obstruction. This is a severe condition and must be treated by a veterinarian.

Vomiting

This medical problem is included because it is so intimately intertwined with nutrition in general. The diagnoses of and causes of vomition in reptiles are essentially the same as those observed in higher vertebrates, but also include causes that are seen exclusively in reptiles. Improper environmental temperature; infectious and/or metabolic disease; parasitism; plant intoxications; putrefaction of ingested material; foreign bodies or ulcerative lesions within the gastrointestinal tract; abscesses; tumors either involving the walls or impinging upon the walls of the gastrointestinal organs; and mere gorging are but some of the myriad number of causes for an iguana to vomit. A proper diagnosis requires obtaining a thorough

71

history and evaluation of captive husbandry practices. Diagnostic radiography or other imaging techniques, microscopic examination of gastric content specimens, and direct fiberoptic endoscopy, with or without simultaneous gastric biopsy, are diagnostic options which may reveal the cause of chronic vomiting. Analysis of the feces may disclose severe gastrointestinal parasitism.

An adequately warm ambient temperature must be provided when feeding captive reptiles. The underlying reason for this is that it permits and even enhances the proper digestion and assimilation of ingested food. This process is linked to several temperature-dependent digestive pancreatic, gastric and intestinal enzymes. Low environmental temperature does not permit internal body temperature sufficient to support digestion. The food simply putrefies and is soon vomited.

Handling a lizard soon after it has eaten often results in the food being regurgitated. This behavior may be a defensive mechanism and has evolved to discourage predators.

Diarrhea

Severe diarrhea is an uncommon problem in captive reptiles. When loose stools are passed by an animal, they should be examined for the presence of disease-causing protozoa and worms. Remember, it is entirely normal for iguanas to have some protozoa in their feces; these microorganisms are essential for normal digestive processes to occur. If these tests reveal disease-causing organisms, appropriate medication should be administered together with supportive therapy by a veterinarian. If none of these organisms is found to be responsible for producing the abnormally soft stools, appropriate dosages of Kaopectate® (Upjohn), Kaopectate Concentrate (Upjohn), Pectolin (EVSCO), etc., can be administered to help relieve the condition. Dosages are directly related to the size and weight of the individual animal.

Sometimes loose stools are the result of the reptile's diet. For example, cucumbers and melons often induce very soft feces. Merely changing the diet to a less moisture-laden food may resolve the diarrhea. Adding pelleted ground alfalfa to the diet often firms the stools dramatically.

With continued diarrhea, the patient may become dehydrated and vital electrolyte imbalances can develop. Severe dehydration and resultant electrolyte imbalances should be managed by the administration of replacement fluid and electrolyte solutions by a veterinarian.

The causes and treatment for vomiting were discussed in the previous section. Because the physiological effects of diarrhea and vomiting can be serious, every effort should be made to diagnose and treat these disturbances early, specifically, and aggressively. Moreover, because some particularly virulent disease-causing organisms can induce both of these disorders simultaneously, a definitive diagnosis is important to reduce the likelihood of horizontal transmission within an animal collection or colony.

Bloating (Tympany)

The production of excessive intestinal gas is most often observed in herbivorous or omnivorous lizards that have ingested food items containing readily fermentable fruit sugars or other substances upon which gastrointestinal microflora subsist. This condition often follows a too rapid change of a diet high in fiber to one containing a higher percentage of metabolizable carbohydrates. Typically, the affected lizard has a grossly observable swelling of its abdomen. This condition can prove fatal if the lungs are compressed by the expanded gastrointestinal organs. Open-mouth breathing and respiratory difficulties are common. Occasionally, the animal vomits, but this is not an invariable characteristic of tympany. If vomiting occurs, the distressed lizard may inhale its vomitus.

Treatment for bloating consists of administering a gas-dissolving agent such as simethicone. There are several nonprescription liquid products which contain this agent and each can easily be delivered via a stomach tube. As mentioned previously, Mylicon® (Stuart) or Riopan Plus II® have proven particularly efficacious. Where deemed appropriate, a veterinarian can inject a modest dose of neostigmine or physostigmine to gently stimulate intestinal motility and, thus, help relieve the retention of gas.

Encouraging the affected animal to exercise may aid in the passage of excessive intestinal gas. Any foods that are linked to bloating must be excluded from the diet. If the signs of excessive gas persist, consult a veterinarian.

Disorders of Blood Sugar

Iguanas, like other animals, convert their food to more readily assimilated constituents. During this metabolic process, complex carbohydrates, particularly cellulose, are changed to simple sugars which can be more easily utilized for energy conversion. Occasionally, inborn or acquired metabolic defects occur which halt or impede these vital processes. Some plants contain substances that specifically attack and destroy the pancreatic cells that normally make insulin. When enough of these cells have been destroyed, the amount of glucose in the blood rises to abnormal levels and diabetes ensues. Although uncommon, diabetes mellitus occurs in iguanas, just as it does in human beings. Once diagnosed, the treatment for diabetes is identical to that used in people, and consists of injections of insulin in appropriate amounts and given at specific times. It is extremely important to maintain a normal dietary intake for these diabetic lizards because the insulin reduces the amount of glucose in the blood. If a source of glucose is not present, the insulin will reduce blood glucose to dangerously low levels which can be fatal. Uncontrolled diabetes often leads to kidney, heart and circulatory failure, blindness, and premature death. Thus, successful treatment for diabetes demands close cooperation between you and your veterinarian.

Under conditions of severe stress, iguanas may suffer from low blood sugar levels. Rarely, this low blood sugar level can occur as a result of a tumor of the pancreas whose cells secrete abnormal amounts of insulin. In either case, this disorder is called *hypoglycemia*, and usually is signaled by "fainting" or severe weakness. The animal's pupils may become and remain dilated even under brilliant illumination. This condition is diagnosed by determining that the lizard's blood sugar is abnormally low. If stress is the underlying cause, the treatment is to give oral or injectable glucose to raise the blood sugar level to within its normal range and remove the cause of the stress. If a pancreatic tumor is responsible, surgery is required, but the prognosis for full recovery is guarded. The differential diagnosis of all of these conditions requires the skills of a veterinarian experienced in working with iguanas.

Coprophagy

The consumption of stools is unusual in most reptiles but, in some species of iguanas, it is entirely normal behavior in hatchlings. As mentioned earlier, newly hatched iguanas acquire the vital fermentative bacteria and protozoa that actually digest the cellulose-rich plant material that is ingested by these lizards. Coprophagy becomes abnormal behavior in older iguanas that already possess an adequate intestinal microflora. When it does occur in older animals, the feces eaten are usually not those of the animal that is ingesting them but, rather, those of other creatures who have defecated within the enclosure.

Most, but not all, intestinal roundworms, tapeworms and flukes are rather host-specific. However, there is an obvious opportunity for the horizontal transmission of disease-causing bacteria, fungi, viruses, protozoa, and worms from an infected or infested animal to cage mates, particularly if they are of the same or closely related species. Many parasitic worms and protozoa are characterized by their direct or indirect multihost life cycles, and may be furnished with the required host when an animal consumes the stools of another.

Coprophagy should be discouraged by strict attention to hygiene and avoidance of overcrowded conditions.

Sauromalus obesus

CHAPTER 6

MISCELLANEOUS INFECTIONS AND INFECTIOUS DISEASES

All lizards are susceptible to infection with fungal, bacterial, and viral disease agents. When kept under hygienic conditions free from overcrowding, stresses induced by improper environmental temperature and territorial disputes, and fed a nutritious diet, iguanas tend to be hardy creatures in captivity. However, when they are kept in filthy enclosures and subjected to overcrowding, maintained at suboptimal temperatures, fed a poor diet, or harried by dominant adult males, these lizards' health can degenerate rapidly.

The reasons for this decline are manifold: cages soiled with feces and spoiled food are breeding grounds for a variety of disease causing microorganisms; overcrowding imposes severe physical and psychic stress; and, as iguanas climb over each other, their filth contaminated claws penetrate the skin of those upon whom they climb and serve efficiently to inoculate bacteria and fungi into the soft tissues underneath the skin. Abscesses soon form. Given the opportunity to do so, bacteria from these localized infections may gain access to the circulatory system and become widely disseminated to internal organs such as the liver, spleen, lungs, brain, etc. Abscesses, by their very nature, tend to be "walled-off" by inflammatory tissue that may effectively isolate the causative microorganisms from the beneficial effects of antibiotics and immune products. Thus, these infections are permitted to grow and extend to adjacent tissues unimpeded. It is for this reason that when multiple abscesses are found in an iguana, it is a cause for serious concern and aggressive veterinary medical intervention. Abscesses often are found around the eyelids, ear openings, limbs, trunk or, less commonly, on the tail (Figure 25 a–d). Usually, they are round, bulging above the surrounding skin surface, and feel firm when touched with a finger.

Figure 25 a–d—see pages 90 & 91

Effective treatment consists of incision and drainage of the abscess contents, removal of the lining of the abscess cavity, flushing and packing the cavity with an antiseptic and appropriate medication, and administering an effective antibiotic whose dosage depends upon the lizard's body weight. These procedures are best left to a veterinarian. Fortunately, today there is an ever-increasing cadre of well-trained veterinarians who are interested in treating reptiles as patients and an armamentarium of highly effective antibiotics and anesthetics that are remarkably safe and efficient. Any unusual lump or bump, swelling, discoloration, or "sore" should be examined and evaluated by a veterinarian skilled in treating nondomestic animals. Veterinary care for iguanas is not a province for pet shop proprietors, zoo keepers, or biology teachers. Similar to treating dogs, horses, swine, goats, or wombats, medical care for lizards should not be left to amateurs. Given the opportunity to extend to deeper tissues and structures, abscesses may eventually cause the loss of limbs, eyes, ears, tail—or the life—of an inadequately treated iguana.

Digits and tails sometimes appear to spontaneously die and drop off. Some of these instances are the result of trauma such as having the body part caught beneath a falling branch or heavy stone. Occasionally, a tiny ringlet of retained shed skin dries and serves as a tourniquet, stopping normal blood flow to the toe, finger or, less often, a portion of the tail. Cage "furniture" should be properly installed so that falling branches, tree trunks, or stones cannot shift and crush the lizards. Careful inspection of the iguanas during and after their periodic skin molts should become routine in order that any retained pieces found can be soaked and softened so that they can be easily removed before they cause inadvertent amputation.

Respiratory infections are not particularly common in iguanas. When they do occur, usually there is a history of the lizard being chilled. The major signs are *excessive* sneezing, obvious difficulty in breathing, abnormally rapid respiratory rate, bubbling or frothy secretions coming from the mouth or nostrils, lethargy, loss of appetite, and the nonspecific sign seen during many diseases: a change from normal bright hues to darker, more somber colors. Some of these same clinical manifestations can be seen with internal parasitism also; thus, consultation with a veterinarian is highly recommended.

Rapid respiration, lethargy, inappetence, and color change can also be seen with profound anemia. The major causes for anemia in iguanas are gastrointestinal parasitism, malaria, and leukemia. Because some iguanas sold through pet dealers today are captive bred, the incidence of severe intestinal parasitism and malaria are greatly reduced when compared to wild-caught lizards who have been exposed to the natural vectors or reservoir hosts for these parasites. Gastrointestinal parasites are diagnosed through the laboratory analysis of feces; malarial parasitism is determined through the microscopic examination of stained specimens of blood. This test requires only a small volume of blood and it should not pose a threat to your iguana.

Gastrointestinal parasitism is treated by administering specific drugs which kill the worms; malaria is treated with specific antimalarial agents that must be given under the supervision of a veterinarian. Often, even the presence of a low level of infection with malarial parasites does not necessarily call for aggressive treatment because these organisms may not pose a significant threat to the animal; this depends upon the type of parasites found, their number, and the overall response to the infection by the lizard. In those instances where severe anemia is present, treatment with an antimalarial drug is indicated. (See Frye, 1991a.)

A herpes virus has been isolated from common green iguanas, and has been characterized and found to be related to a form of leukemia. While unusual, this disease is becoming better understood and is relatively easy to diagnose. At this time, there is no effective treatment known. The signs of this disease are loss of appetite, lethargy, usually a paleness of the tongue and oral mucous membranes and, often, a yellow hue to the whites of the eyes and oral mucous membranes. This disease is believed to be infectious and all exposed animals should be isolated and/or destroyed so that they do not pose a health threat to uninfected lizards. Treatment with acyclovir (Zovirax®) at 90 mg/kg daily has been effective.

Dipsosaurus dorsalis

CHAPTER 7

PARASITES

ENDOPARASITES

Roundworms and tapeworms are the most commonly encountered internal helminths (worms). Some of these worms possess direct life cycles, e.g., they are transmitted from one iguana to another, usually via fecal contamination. Others utilize other creatures as intermediate hosts before developing in the body of an iguana. Many worms inhabit the gastrointestinal tract; others, particularly flukes, parasitize the liver and gallbladder. Additionally, degenerate wormlike arachnids, called pentastomids, usually parasitize other organs such as the lungs. Infestation with most of these parasitic worms is diagnosed by routine microscopic examination of the iguana's feces.

Another group of worms that infest wild-caught iguanas are the filarids. Adult filarid worms may live within specific organs, or they may be found free within the body cavity where they mate and produce living young, called *microfilariae*, which gain access to the circulating blood. Taken up with a blood meal by a biting arthropod such as a mosquito, the tiny microfilariae are transmitted to other susceptible iguanas. Therefore, the diagnosis of filariasis rests upon finding their characteristic microfilariae during the microscopic examination of stained blood specimens. Fortunately, a variety of effective parasiticides are available which can safely and efficiently treat most internal helminth parasites. These drugs should be administered by a veterinarian skilled in herpetological medicine.

ECTOPARASITES

External parasites occasionally are found on iguanas, most often, mites and ticks. Several species of mites infest reptiles, but all of them can be treated identically. The infested lizard should be placed in a vessel containing tepid water just deep enough to cover its back. A majority of the mites will be drowned after approximately 30 minutes. This soaking treatment may be repeated daily, but usually only two or three are sufficient to accomplish eradication. An insecticidal spray that is safe for kittens and puppies can be used, but should not be sprayed directly upon the lizard's skin; rather, spray a modest amount onto a clean cloth, diaper, or sanitary napkin and use this to apply the agent to the iguana's skin. The entire interior of the cage, including all cage "furniture" and litter, also must be either discarded or thoroughly cleansed in boiling water.

Individual ticks can be removed by applying a small volume of alcohol to them while they are attached to the skin. After a few moments, they should be grasped firmly with a tweezers, without crushing them, and detached. Alternatively, they can be removed by using a dull knife blade using a scraping motion.

Cyclura macleayi

CHAPTER 8

MISCELLANEOUS CONDITIONS

Abrasions to the skin covering the front of the iguana's nose, or *rostrum*, are relatively common. They result from the lizard continually scraping its nose and chin against the surfaces of the cage or enclosure. Often, this behavior occurs because the animal fails to perceive the restraining walls of its glass or plastic cage, or screened walls of those which are covered with coarse hardware cloth. Transparent walls should be furnished with a wide strip of opaque plastic or dark paint so as to form a visual barrier to the iguana, thus inhibiting attempts to escape or habitually rub against the cage surfaces. Hardware cloth should be replaced either with a smooth surface or covered with a nonabrasive material. (See Frye, 1991a.)

Treatment of these abrasions consists of gentle cleansing of the lesion and application of a soothing medication such as Neosporin® cream or Polysporin® ointment. Medication should be continued until the skin has healed completely. If the abrasion is quite deep, the liquid bandage, NewSkin®, can be applied over the site to help protect it from further trauma while it heals.

Thermal burns usually occur after lizards come into direct or indirect contact with heating devices such as light bulbs, resistance heated electrical stones or blocks, or subsurface heating pads which produce too much heat. The signs of thermal burning consist of discoloration of the burned part, usually the belly or inner aspects of the limbs. Blistering may or may not be apparent. In some instances, the dorsal spines and eyelids may be lost after they have become overheated by overhead infrared heating devices.

Treatment of thermal burns is similar to that for rostral abrasions, i.e., cleansing and topical medication with the same products noted above. In cases of more severe burning, prompt veterinary attention should be sought.

Overheating (*hyperthermia*) usually occurs as a result of malfunctioning heating devices or confinement in closed transparent cages exposed to sunlight. Signs of heat stress are profound lethargy to the point of collapse and unresponsiveness, and a nonspecific change of skin color to a somber grayish- or brownish-green. Treatment should be directed at removing the lizard from the source of heat and cooling it under tepid water. In severe cases, the iguana should be evaluated and treated by a veterinarian.

Cooling (*hypothermia*), or exposure to abnormally cold environmental temperatures, produces more subtle effects. Once a reptile is exposed to severe and prolonged cooling, its immunity to infection is greatly diminished, thus making it more prone to a variety of bacterial, fungal, and viral diseases. Treatment depends largely upon the signs that the lizard is exhibiting, but includes warming its environment to a range of between 26.7°–31.1° C (80°–88° F). If there is evidence of infection, it must be treated aggressively with appropriate antibiotic therapy.

Electrocution occurs from contact with improperly functioning electrical heating and lighting devices installed in the cage; sometimes, the electrical cord of a heating stone cracks and permits stray currents to injure cage inhabitants.

Signs of electrocution are sudden and profound collapse or paralysis with or without a skin color change, although visible charring or discoloration may be seen as discrete lesions. *CAUTION: UNPLUG THE DEVICE BEFORE TOUCHING THE VICTIM OF ANY SUSPECTED ELECTROCUTION!* After the power has been disconnected, remove the lizard and seek veterinary care immediately.

Moist or dry dermatitis is seen occasionally in captive iguanas. This condition may appear as patches of obviously abnormal skin whose color differs markedly from the surrounding epidermis. These sites may be either dry and unyielding to finger pressure, or they may be moist and weeping sticky fluid. In either case, veterinary care should be sought.

Limb, rib, tail, and spinal fractures occur principally from two major sources: (1) as a result of underlying nutritional deficiencies that cause the bones to be soft and, (2) from falls or being caught beneath falling branches or tree trunks within the cage. Minor fractures of the digits can be easily splinted so that the fingers or toes are wrapped with soft and pliant cast padding materials over a ball of clean cotton. More serious limb or tail fractures should be evaluated by a veterinarian. In some cases, these fractures can be treated adequately with external splintage; others require surgical implantation of fixation appliances. Some tail fractures, if they are not complete, can be splinted so that the damaged tissues can reunite. If the tail breaks off very close to the body, it may not regenerate, but if the break is farther down the organ, it usually will regrow over a period of several months to a year or more. The new tail begins as a rounded bulge

Figure 2. Between the two lateral eyes is the parietal eye, a photosensitive organ with which iguanas help regulate their basking activities. Photo by Dr. F. L. Frye.

Figure 5. Hatching green iguana. Once the lizard has slit its eggshell, it may remain within the opened egg for as long as a day. Photo courtesy of Dr. Gunther Köhler.

Figure 6. Young green iguana displaying a fully extended dewlap. Photo by Dr. F. L. Frye.

Figure 9 a. Many iguanas become accustomed to being hand fed. While it may appear to be appealing, this practice can result in lizards who may refuse to feed from a container. Photo by W. Townsend.

Figure 9 b. Many iguanas become accustomed to being hand fed. While it may appear to be appealing, this practice can result in lizards who may refuse to feed from a container. Photo by W. Townsend.

Figure 12 a–b. Photographs of the splendid outdoor iguana compound at the San Diego Zoological Park. The environment is surrounded by a low, smooth-sided concrete wall and is planted with mature mimosa and other trees which provide edible forage as well as vital shade and sites where individual lizards can exercise their territorial imperatives. Photos by W. Townsend.

Figure 13. Radiograph of a chuckawalla whose stomach and intestines contain rocks and stones that it ingested from its cage environment. Photo by Dr. F. L. Frye.

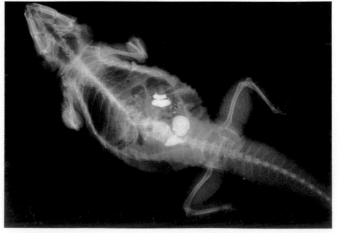

Figure 14 a. Salt crystals have accumulated around the nostrils of this iguana. Photo by Dr. F. L. Frye.

Figure 16. An example of edible vegetables, blossoms, sprouts, and bean cake that comprise a suitably nutritious diet for many captive iguanine species. Photo by W. Townsend.

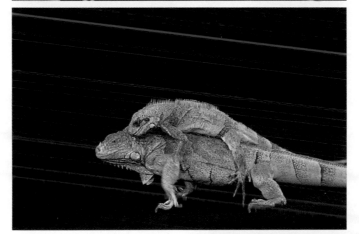

Figure 18. Occasionally, even small male iguanas will attempt to mate with much substantially larger females of their species. Photo by W. Townsend.

Figure 19. While maneuvering a compliant female during the process of copulation, the successful male holds his mate with his teeth. Photo by W. Townsend.

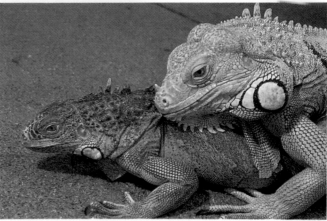

Figure 20 a–b. After one or more bouts of courtship and mating, females often show the effects of having been bitten by their suitors. Photos by Dr. F. L. Frye.

Figure 21. Term gravid female green iguana. Note how the eggs are distending the belly wall. Photo by Dr. F. L. Frye.

Figure 22. A female green iguana with a portion of her clutch of eggs. Photo by W. Townsend.

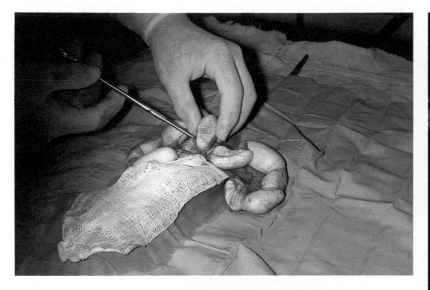

Figure 23. Intraoperative photograph of an ovariohysterectomy (spay) operation on an iguana. The two egg-filled oviducts have been brought to the exterior and are being ligated prior to being removed, and the closure of the abdominal cavity. Photo by Dr. F. L. Frye.

Figure 24 a–c. Examples of anatomic deformities induced by metabolic bone disease. Note the swollen and fore-shortened jaws and limb bones. Photos by Dr. F. L. Frye.

Figure 24 d–e. Examples of anatomic deformities induced by metabolic bone disease. Note the swollen and foreshortened jaws and limb bones. Photos by Dr. F. L. Frye.

Figure 25 a–b. Examples of abscesses in iguanas. These inflammatory lesions can, at times, become quite large. Photos by Dr. F. L. Frye.

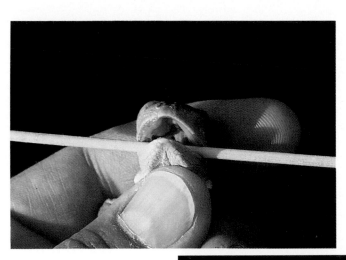

Figure 25 c–d. Examples of abscesses in iguanas. These inflammatory lesions can, at times, become quite large. Photos by Dr. F. L. Frye.

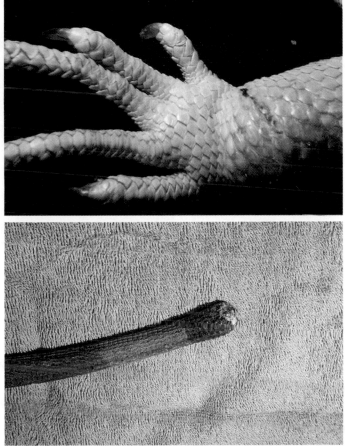

Figure 26 a–b. Although tail breakage in iguanine lizards usually results in a somewhat shorter and less colorful regrown tail, sometimes the regrown organ grows in an opposite direction or may even develop one or more branches or spurs. In some instances, the tail fails to regenerate and only heals as a rounded stump. Photos by Dr. F. L. Frye.

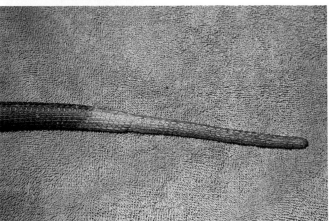

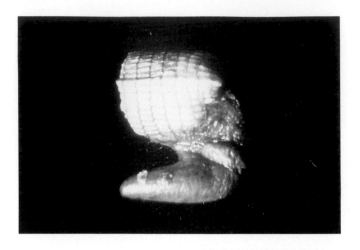

Figure 26 c–e. Although tail breakage in iguanine lizards usually results in a somewhat shorter and less colorful regrown tail, sometimes the regrown organ grows in an opposite direction or may even develop one or more branches or spurs. In some instances, the tail fails to regenerate and only heals as a rounded stump. Photos by Dr. F. L. Frye.

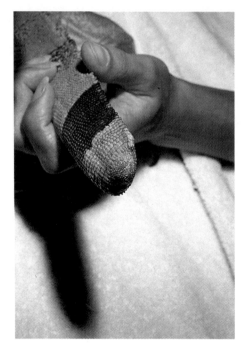

Figure 29. Male iguana grasping its owner's glove in the manner in which it would restrain a female; the lizard is also masturbating on the inanimate object. Photo credit: Betty Jean Lifton.

**Figure 26 a–e—see
pages 91 & 92**

which soon elongates and tapers toward its end (Figure 26 a & b). The new tail will be less colorful and the scales may be irregular but, nevertheless, it can function fully as a balance organ. Sometimes, a regrown tail will grow in an abnormal direction or even have two or several branches (Figure 26 c & d). Occasionally, after several regeneration cycles, a broken tail merely rounds over and does not grow to a tapered point (Figure 26 e).

Iguanas sometimes will ingest foreign bodies which can, because of their nature, cause intoxication, poisoning, or intestinal obstruction. Diagnostic radiography often will disclose the nature of these objects. In some cases, they may be removed without surgery; others will require surgical intervention.

Living in the jungle or on rocky islands, wild iguanas wear their claws down regularly as they walk and climb among the objects in their environment. However, captive lizards living their lives in cages or in household habitats furnished with soft carpeting tend to suffer from overgrowth of their claws. Sometimes, these overly long claws catch in cloth curtains or drapery, and may cause severe injury as the lizard falls from a high perch. Severe overgrowth can lead to deformed toes and infections that result from grossly long claws curving around and penetrating the soft tissues of the feet. Where more than a single iguana is kept in a cage, the lizards may injure each other's skin as they crawl over each other; if their sharp claws puncture the skin, disease-causing bacteria or fungi may be introduced.

The claws can be easily trimmed in smaller lizards with the same nail clippers that we use to groom our own nails; for larger iguanas, a pair of nail clippers used in veterinary practice are used (Figure 27). These

Figure 27. A nail clipper is used to trim the sharp claws of pet iguanas. Photo by W. Townsend.

devices are inexpensive and efficiently shorten overgrown lizard claws without damaging the softer structures. Only the sharp tips of the claws need be trimmed back. Sometimes a small amount of bleeding is caused by trimming the claw back too far. This bleeding usually can be controlled by applying pressure to the bleeding claw with a cotton ball; in cases where more severe bleeding occurs, the application of a styptic pencil, usually employed for staunching the bleeding from minor shaving cuts, may help to stop the blood flow.

Bladder stones occur occasionally in lizards just as they do in humans. Usually, they are diagnosed with radiography (x-ray imaging) (Figure 28). Their development often can be traced to diets overly rich in animal protein; some form spontaneously. Although they may occasionally be passed from the urinary bladder, more often they must be removed surgically by a veterinary surgeon. Adequate access to fresh water and a diet of green and calcium-rich leaves will help prevent the development of these objects.

As iguanas grow older, the whites of their eyes become mildly pigmented and appear pale brown. This is an entirely normal consequence of aging.

SEXUAL AGGRESSION BY IGUANAS TOWARD THEIR OWNERS

After several years of feeding, routine care, and close attention by its owner, it is not unusual for a close bond to form between a maturing male iguana and its female owner. This is not to suggest that a similarly firm bond is not created between female iguanas and their male owners, but in the case of mature male iguanas and their women owners, sometimes an abnormally strong attachment is formed. The senior author has now documented 26 cases of unprovoked sexual aggression in which male iguanas have displayed more than casual interest in their female owners. (For the first 18 cases, see Frye, Mader, and Centofanti, 1991.)

Most often, this aggression takes the form of stereotyped courtship displays commencing with head nodding, dewlap extension, chasing, biting and hemipenial protrusion. In some of these cases, masturbation on objects and even ejaculation by these iguanas have been observed by their astonished owners (Figure 29).

Most of these instances have involved relationships between iguanas obtained when very young and women of child-bearing age who have had unusually close contact with their pet iguanas. The owners fed their lizards at the same table where humans dine, showered or bathed with them, even

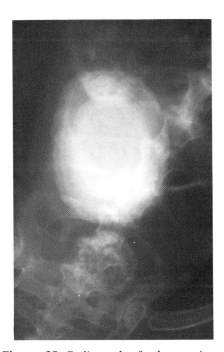

Figure 28. Radiograph of a large urinary bladder stone in a spiny-tailed iguana that was successfully removed surgically. Photo by Dr. F. L. Frye.

Figure 29—see page 92

permitted the lizards to sleep in or on the same bed. Essentially all cases involved adult male iguanas who were raised as "only children" without contact with other iguanas, either male or female.

In every case investigated to the date of this writing, each of these aggravated displays occurred while the woman owner has been menstruating or ovulating. The most likely cause for this remarkable behavior would be a *pheromone*, or chemical cue, that is secreted during the human menstrual cycle that can be perceived by an iguana and closely mimics a similar scent-like substance that is secreted by female or, perhaps *male*, iguanas and, thereby, acts as a stimulus for sexual aggression.

Although there is no specific treatment for this sexual aggression directed against human owners, several things can be done to ameliorate it. Simply confining the offending iguana to a cage or other enclosure will make aggression much less likely to occur. If this remedy is not acceptable, surgical intervention in the form of castration should be considered. Alternatively, injectable female hormone in the long-acting "depot" form can be administered at intervals which will greatly diminish sexual displays and aggression.

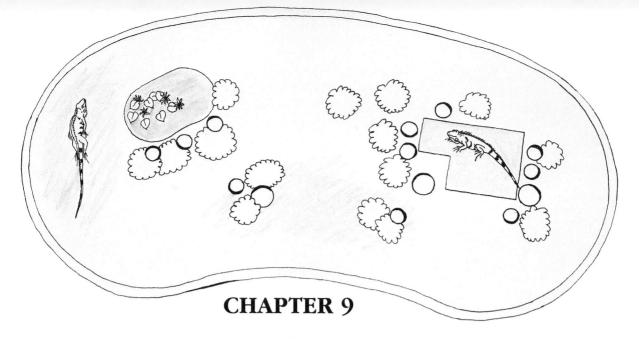

CHAPTER 9

WENDY'S OBSERVATIONS

In this section I am going to tell about the green iguanas with whom I have been sharing my home. Most of these lizards were acquired as damaged or ailing animals, but with compassionate care quickly became fine pets. It is hoped that telling of my iguanas' behavior and activities will be interesting and sometimes endearing, and that many lessons about iguana care will be derived from these anecdotes. The accompanying table (6) of iguana names and vital data is provided for ease in following the progress of each of these lizards.

For my tenth birthday gift, I was taken to a pet shop and allowed to pick out my first iguana, who later became known as "Wiener." (She was named by my six-year-old cousin, who distorted the word "iguana" into "Wiener.") Wiener was the saddest of the group of juveniles at the pet shop. I wanted to "rescue" the lizard, which is why I chose an apparently weak animal.

Weeks later, I purchased "Iggly," a healthy juvenile who became Wiener's companion. These two lizards never mated, perhaps because of insufficient year-round lighting and territory, and the absence of other iguanas. One Christmas, I left town for two weeks with my family. The two iguanas were left in the theoretical care of a sitter who did not replace a heat lamp when it went out. Our home in New York was too cold for the iguanas without the supplementary heat source. Wiener was merely chilled, but Iggly was quite ill. A veterinarian examined the sick iguana and determined that euthanasia would be the kindest treatment.

I purchased Skitz from a fellow who was in the habit of continuously playing loud, raucous music within inches of the lizards' cage. Skitz's cage mate had died some weeks earlier. Her housing was filthy and cold, and her diet was lettuce and banana. Skitz is presently healthy, though she should

TABLE 6
Wendy's Experiences with Pet Iguanas

Name	Sex/SVL*	Age When Received	#Years in My Group	Present Status & SVL*
Wiener	F 3″	6 months	10 yrs	Deceased; 14″
Iggly W.	M 4″	hatchling	4 yrs	Deceased; 15″ (e)
Skitz	F 7″	1 yr (?)	5 yrs	Healthy; 10″
Spot	M 6″	1 yr	10 yrs	Healthy; 16″
Peanut	M 4″	2 yrs	7 yrs	Healthy; stunted @ 8″
Pete	M 10″	3 yrs	7 mo	Deceased; 12″
Debra	F 9″	3 yrs	4 yrs	Deceased; 15″
Stumpy	M 8″	2 yrs	2 yrs	Relocated; healthy
Pooky	F 5″	6 mo	7 yrs	Deceased; 14″
Snooky	F 6″	6 mo	9 yrs	Deceased; 15″
E. T.	F 6″	2 yrs	1 yr	Healthy; 13″
Queenie	F 8″	2 yrs	1 yr	Healthy; 13″
Goober	F 3″	hatchling	5 yrs	Healthy; 16″
Fishy	F 7″	10 mo	6 mo	Healthy; 10″
Tiny Thing	? 3″	hatchling	5 mo	Healthy; 4″
Harry	? 3″	hatchling	1 mo	Healthy; 3″

*SVL = snout to vent length in .

be larger. She has not acclimated "emotionally," and remains nervous and fearful, spending much time in a hiding box.

I got Spot from a boy who was keeping the lizard in a bathroom with a light bulb for heat and a branch. Spot's diet had been fruit cocktail, lettuce and hamburger. He had soft, rubbery bones and an "S"-shaped spine. He is now quite large, and has had no health problems.

Peanut belonged to a woman who had been feeding him romaine lettuce, banana and other fruits, with yogurt being the only protein and calcium source. Peanut's keeper had had him for two years, during which time his growth was minimal, probably due to insufficient diet and lack of sunshine (or its substitute). Peanut has grown a meager four inches in five years. His continued lack of growth may be due to stress caused by Spot, though they're kept visually separate most of the time, as well as irreparable damage done during his development. In spite of his poor growth, Peanut feeds well and is active and strong. Spot, on the other hand, has grown very large. Both lizards are the same age, and are sexually mature.

Peanut seems perpetually desirous of mating, but will probably never be accepted by a female. Spot has always wanted to kill Peanut, and flies into a rage at the slightest glimpse of him. As if unaware of his tiny size, Peanut constantly struggles to fight with Spot. Such an encounter would last three seconds ending with Peanut's head pulverized. Peanut is even more eager to mount any female. Given a moment's access to the group (with Spot out of the room), Peanut is right on top of the nearest female, desperately trying to breed. The selective females will have nothing to do with little, inadequate Peanut, and dispatch him quickly with a kick from a back leg. It becomes necessary to remove Peanut from the group for he'll persist in his amorous approaches until his would-be mate seriously injures or kills him.

I adopted Pete and Debra from a man who was keeping these lizards in a mildewy, unclean bathroom. Pete and Debra were underweight, and both had a fungal skin infection which ran the length from forearmpit to midtail. Healthy diet, warm, clean housing and application of Neosporin® to the infected skin helped the two iguanas gain weight and recover in a matter of days. Pete and Debra were given free range of one room while Spot, Pooky, Snooky and I shared another. Pete and Spot were ever aware of each other, and faced off constantly in the "neutral" territory between rooms. Debra insisted on going into Spot's area even after I returned her to Pete's many times. Though Spot never injured Pete, his intimidating presence wore him down. When Debra was 7 years old, she laid 39 eggs and died within 24 hours.

Stumpy came from a couple who fed him cat food and lettuce. This iguana was named for what remained of his tail, which had atrophied, probably after a breakage, and dropped off. He was extremely emaciated and had gnarled, brittle forelimbs. With care, he improved immensely during the first year. The healthier he became, the more he strove to challenge Spot and establish his own territory. Stumpy reached a point when his improvement leveled off as more of his energy was being spent on "normal male activities." Within the second year, I located an excellent new home for him where he could rule and not suffer Pete's fate. I had difficulty parting with Stumpy as he was a remarkably delightful pet. Stumpy's initial adoption and eventual relocation were accomplished through the Southwestern Herpetological Society.

Pooky and Snooky were both healthy youngsters and were gifts from a friend. When Pooky was 5, she laid 36 eggs. One egg gave her difficulty, and was passed three days later, brown and overly large. Before this last egg she was treated with injectable vitamins, an appetite stimulant, electrolyte solution and antibiotic—all recommended by a veterinarian. Two years later, Pooky laid 43 eggs and collapsed despite rehydration and other efforts to replenish her. Snooky produced three annual consecutive batches of eggs with no complications. The fourth pregnancy brought on an oviduct infection. Though she was treated with antibiotics, fluids, tube feedings and surgery, she died.

E.T. and Queenie came via special overnight delivery from an ill-informed, but conscientious, keeper. With their apparent declining health, this keeper wanted to relocate the iguanas. Both were undersized for their age, and both had a couple of swollen joints. E.T. has a severe overbite due to her lower jaw which had softened after having been broken some time before. Both iguanas are wonderful pets, and have been growing rapidly. E.T. has laid 13 eggs while being kept with Peanut but these were not fertile.

E.T. has an immense appetite, and prefers to be hand-fed, particularly because her deformed jaw is a hindrance to a hearty feeding if left alone with a meal.

I obtained Goober as a hatchling from a pet shop. She had a broken arm that none of the employees would deal with. Now she almost out-weighs Spot, though she still has a "trick" wrist where the break had been. Goober is a remarkably outgoing, even aggressive lizard. She will tolerate being petted and picked up only if she's in the "mood." Consistent with Goober's "whimsy," she is always curious and runs over to get in on most every activity in the room. She is a marvelous, impressive lizard—and is sometimes fun to playfully tease.

I bought Fishy from a pet shop at cost because she was too thin, excessively restless, and had a large abscess on her jaw. A tooth had broken, becoming lodged inside her mouth, causing the abscess. The pet shop employees were having difficulty with this, and had actually exacerbated the problem as the entrance to the abscess was inside the mouth and not on the outer lip, where they were lancing. Careful removal of the tooth and abscess were later accomplished and several pureed meals were adminis-tered during recovery. Fishy is presently in excellent condition.

Tiny Thing was the yellow-orange color of a pencil when I obtained him. A few barely green scales indicated that his normal color should be bright green. Tiny had been chewed on by the crickets he was supposed to eat, and there were two conspicuous bites on his back. Pet shop employees had been cramming wax worms down his throat because he wouldn't eat voluntarily. They had to have been certain Tiny would die, because they gave him to me. "Here, you take him. He'll never make it." Tiny was so bad off the proprietor didn't have the conscience to tap me, the bleeding heart, for even a few bucks. (A month earlier I bought Fishy from this shop.) I took the pitiful thread of an iguana home and set him up in a 7-gallon tank with a little potted pothos with trailing vines for his comfort. Before putting Tiny to bed, I soaked him in the bathroom sink in tepid water. This was to remove the fecal staining around his vent, which is typical of sick iguanas. While Tiny soaked, I pureed some papaya, a little kale and marmoset chow, plus enough water to make a thick liquid. After straining the mixture, I drew a 1.0 cc syringe full, with the intention of forcing Tiny to eat. To my surprise, he needed no forcing, and lapped up the meal in its entirety. The next morning, calcium carbonate and NutriCal® were added to his breakfast, and then Tiny and I went outside for some sunshine therapy. Because a little iguana would easily overheat, I put Tiny on a "flotilla" of a kale leaf in a plastic tub of water. Within 20 minutes, the lizard defecated an undigested wax worm. Later, he started turning green. The next day, Tiny ate several sweet, pink flowers from a guava tree (*Psidium* sp.) and pieces of his kale flotilla. It took three days with two putrid bowel movements daily for Tiny to cleanse himself of what he had been fed. Half his diet these days was overripe papaya to help encourage his digestive processes. Three weeks later, Tiny shed his epidermis, and the cricket bites were nearly gone. Neosporin® cream was initially applied to the bites and, later, liquid vitamin E was used on them to serve as an emollient.

Tiny now eats the same food as the other iguanas. With his inquisitive ways and infant-like appearance, Tiny wins the hearts of the people he meets.

For the most part, I have managed to hire acceptable iguana sitters while I travel out of town. During Tiny's recuperation, he made three trips via airplane with me. Because of his need for daily attention, I didn't leave him for the sitter to tend with the other lizards. Being all of three inches SVL and especially fragile, it could hardly be reasonable to sack and box Tiny and put him through as "special baggage." Therefore he traveled in a lightweight cotton sock pinned to my undergarment. I had to be careful not to shoulder a bag or hug a family member closely upon arrival, as Tiny could be crushed. Much of my family finds Tiny's means of travel a source of relative hilarity.

I often forget how healthy Tiny has become, and he has reminded me a few times by nearly slipping away. Though Tiny is exceptionally tame, a sudden movement can cause him to flee. Once I put him to bask on a densely foliated potted bush on a sun deck. A pelican flew overhead, closer than the gulls and terns that had passed earlier, and Tiny dove for cover into the core of the bush. Another time, a more serious incident warned me to keep a better watch on Tiny. My two cats have never paid much attention to the lizards, even little Peanut. It was Tiny's agile movements and wispy tail that were irresistible to one of the cats that nearly killed him.

The responsibility for a pet iguana's injury or death usually rests on the keeper. Finding the piece of Tiny's tail and then his mauled, fur-encrusted, barely living body behind a shelf was a most unpleasant reminder of this. A month later, nearly two inches of his tail had grown back, and the scars were almost gone.

Every spring as I was growing up, our Volkswagen bug was loaded to capacity with "stuff," including a cat, various snakes and lizards and two or more iguanas. Each reptile traveled in his or her own pillow case for the long trip from New York City to Northern Michigan where we spent the summer. Great care was taken to place the animals where they would have ample air circulation and would not overheat or be crushed by shifting objects. The iguanas stayed secure in their pillowcases for the duration of the trip. (Road travels lasting longer than 24 hours require a little time out of the bag for water, though feeding is not recommended until a final destination is reached.)

The iguanas' Michigan home was a large cage in the studio-garage of a cabin on a lake. Each morning, the doors which made up one side of the building were opened, and direct sunlight reached the lizards for much of the day. A spot light bulb in a reflector fixture was set up for added warmth. Throughout the summer, many neighbors from around the lake would come by to look at the iguanas, sometimes asking questions, other times watching quietly. During these summers, I busied myself both with the abundant local wildlife and my own pets. On sunny days, I took the iguanas, one at a time, out on the dock. Wiener especially liked to bask on the bow of a big wooden boat which was anchored nearby. I kept an eye on the lizard as she would dive into the water to cool down, or if she spotted a dog. Wiener could see dogs and people moving a hundred yards away, and if they came closer, she'd flatten out and prepare to dive. The gulls flying overhead did not trouble her once she had grown fairly large. The lake was clear, shallow near shore, and had a fine, sandy bottom which gave good visibility to Wiener's graceful swimming. She usually swam towards shore where she would dig and nibble at the sand. Wild blueberry bushes and dandelions grew there on the beach, and I would pick these for her. Often, Wiener would climb one of the huge pine trees, which I let her do, until her body almost got out of reach.

Michigan nights get cold, especially late in the summer. On these nights (when they were big enough to "kick back" if I rolled over), I put Wiener and Iggly in my sleeping bag so they'd keep warm. Like anything else the iguana becomes accustomed to, they came to expect such night-time accommodations. After Iggly died, Wiener continued to sleep in my bed year-round, lying with limbs extended back against her body, sound asleep by my side. At sunrise, she woke up and found her way to her basking site.

When I went to live in the dormitory at the University of Miami, Florida, pets were not allowed. The biology department was pleased to provide a large wood-and-glass enclosure for Wiener, which I set up with branches and lights. I had a key to the room where she lived, and picked her up almost every night to bring back to my room. Initially, my roommate was a bit fearful of Wiener. Within a week, we were tossing coins over who got to have the lizard for the night. Of course, people knew about the iguana going back and forth from lab to dorm under my jacket, but "looked the other way," because I was a freshman and probably looked as homesick as I was.

When Iggly died, I purchased my first and last wild-caught, adult iguana. He seemed to acclimate, and fed well. Though he appeared physically healthy, much of the time he seemed remote or depressed—until his first summer in Michigan. The very day I took the lizard outside for sunshine and a swim, he went wild when I tried to take him back indoors. He never calmed down that day, and frantically dug at his cage until his nose was bloodied. I slathered on the Neosporin® and put him in a canvas laundry bag in the cool bedroom which faced the woods. I wanted him to "chill out" for an hour while I prepared new accommodations for this wild animal who appeared to have snapped out of his depressed state, probably realizing his captivity and not liking it one bit.

I went to check on the lizard a half hour later. He had torn the canvas bag, torn the screen on the window which faced the deep woods, and was never found despite much searching and posting of signs. For many nights I had miserable fantasies about the unfortunate iguana's demise. If a raccoon, owl, or car didn't get him, the winter did. Oddly, that summer there had been an article in the local newspaper: "The iguana: Man's best friend?" According to the article, several iguanas had been reported to the animal shelter as missing. One lizard was found in a garden, and several people came to claim it.

The most humorous iguana moment my parents recall—and retell—was when Iggly got down from his perch, high-stepped his way into the living room and went on to the kitchen. He approached Felix, our cat, who was eating, and bobbed vigorously, intimidating the cat into abandoning her food. Iggly then ate the cat's meal and promptly returned to his room, while Felix, we and our dozen or so dinner guests looked on. Probably our guests still tell this story now and then, too.

My grandparents have a home in rural Indiana, the cabin in Michigan, and a winter home in the Bahamas. Every year since childhood, I've made no fewer than three trips to visit my family in these places. With some effort, travel and vacations with pet iguanas are possible. Over the years of taking iguanas "on the road" or arranging for their care at home, Iggly's death has been the only tragedy.

Travel abroad with pet iguanas is difficult, if not impossible, but within the United States, iguanas can be transported via airplane with minor inconvenience. When I transplanted from New York to California, I moved six boas, three pythons and five iguanas. Here is the procedure for air travel with iguanas:

Call the airline you're using and tell the agent you need to transport one (spare yourself complications) iguana. The reasons for calling ahead are: (a) there will be a "handling fee" for each "special package"; and, (b) some planes don't have cargo compartments with temperature control. If the airline is notified of your package, they will book you onto a plane with a proper compartment. Transport only one iguana per cloth sack or sturdy pillowcase, with the open end tied shut. Up to three large lizards in their sacks will fit comfortably in a large dog kennel or similar sturdy traveling case with good ventilation. Your lizard's case won't come out on a conveyor with the regular luggage, but will be handled separately. Animals other than cats or dogs are not allowed in the passenger area. Do not put a lizard into any box or bag that will go through the security x-ray.

Because I moved frequently during the first few years while living in California, I had an iguana cage built on wheels. I chose some apartments over others for the sunshine the lizards would receive in their room. In each apartment, I put down indoor-outdoor turf to protect the carpeting. At this point, I will mention that while iguanas are well suited to apartment living, not all landlords will allow them. If renting, it is advised that iguana keepers maintain a "low profile" until it is determined that neighbors and building managers don't mind the lizards. In all but one previous rental, my iguanas were tolerated. Fortunately, I was already planning to move on when I received a 30-day notice: "They go, or you go!" Apparently, a neighbor had seen the lizards basking, and complained to the landlord.

When Goober was little, she and I shared the living room of one apartment while the other lizards had the bedroom. Spot had yet to figure out that Goober was female, so I took care to keep the bedroom door shut, for Spot knew Goober was under the same roof. He could not risk the little iguana mating with one of his females, so he was always alerted to a chance to "eliminate" her, which he got one day when a neighbor came to the door, interrupting a feeding and my attention. A small apartment does not allow sufficient retreat for one lizard being chased by another, so Spot nearly tore Goober's head off. I rinsed the wound with Betadine® and water, and confined the injured lizard to a clean glass tank with paper towel and a water bowl. The next day, the vet came and did excellent stitchwork. One year later, Goober and Spot became "best of friends," and the scar is nearly invisible.

Within a population of wild green iguanas, field biologists have occasionally observed adult females to interrupt and disperse a mating pair. Other than this, there seems to be little evidence to suggest that while female iguanas are selective of the males they will mate with, they don't appear to actively claim and guard chosen males. Within my iguana room, it would seem that Goober may be doing precisely this. During the mating season her aggression towards the three other females is heightened. She is particularly nasty to Queenie. As it has turned out, Queenie was Spot's first "choice," though he will eventually pair with each female in turn. (Over the years, Spot has been in the habit of "starting" with the young ones.) Goober repeatedly drives the females away from both Spot and his primary basking site, and then positions herself close to him, periodically bobbing to assert her claim. When a meal is presented, no competition or aggression is observed as all four lizards eat simultaneously and without event.

The social dynamics—and needs—of a population of iguanas, whether captive or wild, are complex, and shift with the number and maturity of individuals and the season. I am careful to provide sufficient hot spots and retreats for the "bullied" iguanas in the room.

Once Goober escaped to the outdoors while we were living in the Venice Beach area. An indoor search revealed a hole in the wall behind the refrigerator. After six weeks and much searching, Goober turned up on the neighbor's porch, contentedly basking in the morning sun. She appeared to have grown an inch or two. Clearly, the sunshine and choice forage of hibiscus and fig were good for her. Nevertheless, releasing or allowing pet iguanas to roam outdoors unattended is irresponsible and must be discouraged. If your iguana should escape, I have included a few suggestions which may increase the chances for finding your pet:

Look up. An iguana will most likely head up a tree or whatever he can climb, so thoroughly scan treetops and roofs, keeping in mind the iguana's ability to remain motionless and camouflaged. Take regular midday strolls around your home, as your pet may be basking or foraging within yards of where he got out. Be mindful of unusual episodes of dog barking as a clue to an iguana's location.

There is a fair chance a neighbor may come across a stray iguana, so either post a few signs describing the lizard as a harmless pet, or go around and tell neighbors personally. If the lost iguana is of notable size, informing police, humane society and animal control departments shouldn't be disregarded. Check the lost-and-found sections of local newspapers. Also, check with local pet shops as exotic strays are periodically found and taken to one of these.

One is hard pressed to present to a tame pet iguana an object which will frighten him. Even so, it seems each lizard can have his own "pet-peeve." Spot adores blueberries, courteously ruptured and offered by hand, one at a time. (If a blueberry is presented unruptured, Spot mouths it until it bursts.) However, if a dish of berries, more than two, is brought into his view, a violent, fearful flight ensues. This same response is elicited by the bottoms of a pair of my moccasins, which have round black nobs arranged on a pale leather sole. Perhaps he perceives blueberry pairs and dark beads as the eyes of a predator. Goober is indifferent to blueberries, singly or collectively, as are the other iguanas, however, she, alone, responds in a frightened manner to humans with white or gray hair or wearing hats, and sometimes to strangers. Occasionally, I forget about her anxieties and enter the room with a towel wrapped around my wet hair. Goober becomes wide-eyed and flies into the wall, scrambling for escape or cover from whatever the hair-towel represents. Pooky had the same problem with small children. Debra couldn't stand the sight of a snake; but this makes sense, as snakes are natural predators to iguanas. Still, Spot, Goober, Snooky and Pooky have never cared, one way or the other, about snakes. This behavior can probably be explained by some aspect of the imprinting process during each iguana's development. In any case, I wonder what the blueberries, towels, or white-haired people represent that apparently terrify each lizard.

The iguana's eyes are very expressive and telling of his moment-to-moment sensation status. Both the rim of the eyelid and the pupil change shape and dilate, according to wariness, fear, inquisitiveness, anger, hunger and recognition, among other conditions. It is particularly moving to sit quietly and still with a baby iguana and establish eye contact with the little lizard. As he is beginning to get used to the human face, in his eyes, the expression of fear is almost completely replaced by what one might call wonder. When he grows up, his look becomes a look of familiarity and—I hope—contentment.

I never cease to be both entertained and moved by iguanas.

"One touch of nature makes the world kin."

—William Shakespeare

"With their parallel lives, animals offer man a companionship which is different from any offered by human exchange. Different because it is a companionship offered to the loneliness of man as a species."

—John Berger

VOICE OF THE IGUANA

Wendy Townsend

Do you see me?
see these luscious, lush
green strong trees and plants too
Hot sunshine
Sweet tender flowers; delicious air
fine opportunities, too-all around!
Choices—lots to do

I'm very busy
So watch—don't take
I'm not the answer
to your problems.
I can give you something precious,
but it may not be
what you had in mind.

EPILOGUE

We wish to conclude our discussion with the question: Why is conscientious iguana keeping important? Conservation can begin in the home. To further this idea, we have lauded the iguana as a highly adaptive, fine pet and have presented much information on proper, compassionate care. People who have positive experiences with iguana-keeping, or even know others who have, are generally enlightened with respect to conservation.

With conservational and environmental issues becoming more and more critical, increased public awareness of—even affection for—the iguana would be most timely. And preserving the iguana would, of course, mean preserving his various habitats: among them, the rain forest!

We hope, whether people elect to have pet iguanas or not, they will hold these animals in high esteem. This point is beautifully made in the introduction to *Iguanas of the World*:

"These animals, popular in zoos, folklore, and illustrations from the time they were first discovered, deserve study, protection and perhaps even reverence."

In addition to the practical environmental reasons for appreciating the iguana, quite simply, there is enormous value in showing kindness and respect towards *all* animals. Such value can be difficult to measure or define, but becomes evident when one or more healthy, happy iguanas are raised. Pet iguanas are teachers of observation and compassion, and are fascinating fellow animals with which we share the planet.

INTERNATIONAL SPECIAL INTEREST IGUANA GROUPS

Pro Iguana Verde Foundation
Apartado 692-1007
San Jose
Costa Rica
Tel: (506)-31-6756
Fax: (506)-32-1950

Die Arbeitsgemeinschaft für
  Leguane
in der DGHT
Publishes *IGUANA* (in German)
% Dr. Gunther Köhler
Liesingstrasse 11
6450 Hanau 9
Germany
Tel: 011-37-6181/573835

International Iguana Society
Finca Cyclura
Rt 3, Box 328
Big Pine Key, FL 33043
Tel: 1-305-872-9811

Association of Amphibian and
  Reptile Veterinarians
% Dr. Thomas H. Boyer
Deer Creek Animal Hospital
10148 W. Chatfield Avenue
Littleton, CO 80127
1-303-873-4200

DIRECTORY OF HERPETOLOGICAL SOCIETIES OF THE UNITED STATES[1]

ARIZONA

Arizona Herpetological Association
P.O. Box 39127
Phoenix, AZ 85069-9127

[1]Compiled by *Reptile and Amphibian Magazine* and *Herpetological Review*.

National Turtle & Tortoise Society
P.O. Box 9806
Phoenix, AZ 85068-9806

Southern Arizona Herpetological Association
% Tom Boyden
4521 West Mars Street
Tucson, AZ 85704

Tucson Herpetological Society
P.O. Box 31531
Tucson, AZ 85751-1531

ARKANSAS

Arkansas Herpetological Society
% Floyd Perk
Route 2, Box 16
Hensley, AK 72065

CALIFORNIA

American Federation of Herpetoculturists
P.O. Box 1131
Lakeside, CA 92040

Bay Area Amphibian & Reptile Society
Palo Alto Junior Museum
1451 Middlefield Road
Palo Alto, CA 94301

California Turtle & Tortoise Society
P.O. Box 7300
Van Nuys, CA 91409-7300

Island Empire Herpetological Society
San Bernardino County Museum
2024 Orange Tree Lane
Redlands, CA 92373